T0195689

Lifestyle of
A Child in God

T.S. WILLIAMS

WESTBOW
PRESS®
A DIVISION OF THOMAS NELSON
& ZONDERVAN

WestBow Press books may be ordered through booksellers or by contacting:

WestBow Press
A Division of Thomas Nelson & Zondervan
1663 Liberty Drive
Bloomington, IN 47403
www.westbowpress.com
844-714-3454

Because of the dynamic nature of the Internet, any web addresses or links contained in this book may have changed since publication and may no longer be valid. The views expressed in this work are solely those of the author and do not necessarily reflect the views of the publisher, and the publisher hereby disclaims any responsibility for them.

Any people depicted in stock imagery provided by Getty Images are models, and such images are being used for illustrative purposes only. Certain stock imagery © Getty Images.

Interior Image Credit: Tia-Che, Sahara-Belle & Jae-Lauren Williams

Scripture taken from the New King James Version® Copyright © 1982 by Thomas Nelson. Used by permission. All rights reserved.

ISBN: 978-1-6642-7742-7 (sc)
ISBN: 978-1-6642-7743-4 (hc)
ISBN: 978-1-6642-7741-0 (e)

Library of Congress Control Number: 2022916445

Print information available on the last page.

WestBow Press rev. date: 09/27/2022

CONTENTS

Introduction

Lifestyle of A Child in God, is a summary of work taught to children from age 5 and upwards in our church's youth department over a period of one year. The illustrations were done at that time by my three daughters: Tia-Che, 13; Sahara-Belle, 10; and Jae-Lauren, 8. This book has its basis in the tabernacle and the priests within it. However, it also incorporates scriptures from the New Testament.

The focus of this book is how to have a real relationship with God that is rooted inside a person.

The lessons are written in first person from the child's point of view, and the stories that accompany the lesson are about children. These stories teach from a perspective of the physical first and then the spiritual. It was designed so that those reading could understand spiritual applications by first understanding physical applications.

This concept is based on what Jesus did when He taught those around Him. He used examples of physical things which had spiritual meanings, such as when Jesus spoke of the importance of heaven in Matthew 13:44:

> Again, the kingdom of heaven is like treasure hidden in a field, which a man found and hid; and for joy over it he goes and sells all that he has and buys that field.

Jesus warned His disciples to be careful of what teaching they accepted as truth:

Now when His disciples had come to the other side, they had forgotten to take bread. Then Jesus said to them, "Take heed and beware of the leaven of the Pharisees and the Sadducees." And they reasoned among themselves, saying, "It is because we have taken no bread." (Matthew 16:5–7)

"How is it you do not understand that I did not speak to you concerning bread?—but to beware of the leaven of the Pharisees and Sadducees." Then they understood that He did not tell them to beware of the leaven of bread, but of the doctrine of the Pharisees and Sadducees. (Matthew 16:11–12)

Lifestyle of A Child in God was written in obedience to God, who has given all that is contained within it and taught me much through it. My hope is that this work touches every heart and leads everyone to a deeper relationship with Jesus, the author and finisher of our faith.

1

Be Willing

The tabernacle is a place where God wants to dwell or make His home. I am to be that tabernacle—a place where God lives. Looking at the physical tabernacle during the time of Moses helps me see how I can become a "home" for God to live in.

> "I will dwell among the children of Israel and will be their God. And they shall know that I am the LORD their God, who brought them up out of the land of Egypt, that I may dwell among them. I am the LORD their God." (Exodus 29:45–46)

The first thing I can see about the physical tabernacle is that it was built with materials that were *willingly* given.

This teaches me that I need to be *willing*, to have a good attitude and be happy in the giving and doing of all the Lord has called me to give and do, such as reading His Word, praying, cleaning up, doing schoolwork, and sharing with others.

The types of things that I should be willing to give and do take time, strength, energy, thought, and understanding.

Then the Lord spoke to Moses, saying: "Speak to the children of Israel, that they bring me an offering. From everyone who gives it willingly with his heart you shall take my offering." (Exodus 25:1–2)

Sheila's First Art Class

Sheila was 6 years old when her mother took her to her first art class so she could learn how to paint beautiful pictures. At first, Sheila was so excited that she jumped up and down. She would be attending art class!

But when Sheila got there and saw the boys and girls, easels, and boards, she felt afraid. She thought she might not paint well and the other children might laugh at her.

Sheila held on tightly to her mother and did not want to stay with Mrs Kilt, the art instructor. But after a while, Mrs Kilt, with her warm smiles and bright eyes, was able to get Sheila to stay.

Soon, Sheila had her art apron on and was sitting behind an easel.

Everyone watched as Mrs Kilt put a beautiful sunflower on the table in front of them. Then she painted the flowers on the canvas so all the children would have an idea of what to do. Sheila enjoyed hearing Mrs Kilt speak about what to do and watching her paint.

Then it was Sheila's turn to paint, but she was unsure of what to do. Sheila still tried. But she was sad that her painting did not look like Mrs Kilt's painting.

Sheila did not want to paint anymore. She got so upset that she knocked her paints and paintbrushes to the floor. She was not willing to paint anymore.

Mrs Kilt picked up the paints and brushes and cleaned up the floor. Then she sat next to Sheila. She told Sheila that when she was a little girl learning to paint for the first time, she too was very scared and wanted to give up.

Mrs Kilt told Sheila that if she had given up, she would not have been able to paint the sunflower or teach others what to do.

Sheila looked up at Mrs Kilt, smiled, and said, "I'm sorry for throwing the paints to the floor."

Mrs Kilt asked, "Would you be willing to try again?"

Sheila said, "Yes, Mrs Kilt."

Mrs Kilt said, "Do you know what it means to be willing?"

Sheila was not sure what it meant, so Mrs Kilt helped her understand. She pulled Sheila close and said, "To be willing means you do your best without getting angry or upset. To be willing means you want to do something and that you're happy as you're doing it."

Sheila understood and said, "Yes, Mrs Kilt, I am willing to paint again. I will do my best, and I'll be happy while I am doing it."

Mrs Kilt brought fresh paint and clean brushes to Sheila, and Sheila tried her best to paint the sunflower. She enjoyed herself even though her painting was not looking exactly the same as the one Mrs Kilt had done. Sheila learnt that to have a willing heart was to have a happy heart.

Baron's Days at School

Baron liked going to school. He liked his teachers. He liked playing with his friends at playtime. He also liked art time. But he did not like when it was time to write in his book. He did not like when it was time to read.

Baron's teacher Mr Tax tried hard to get him to do the work, but Baron did not want to do any work. He was not willing to do any work. When it was time to write, he let his pencil roll around on the table until it fell to the floor. After Baron got tired of picking up his pencil, he would look out the window at the birds on the branches in the trees.

One day, Mr Tax asked Baron why he did not want to do his classwork. Baron did not know what to say. He thought about it. He did not like to work because his fingers got tired of holding his pencil. Sometimes he did not want to work because he really did not understand what to do on his worksheet. He was too scared to ask Mr Tax for help. And sometimes Baron did not want to work because he wanted to play instead.

Baron looked up at Mr Tax and told him what he was thinking. Mr Tax knew how he could help. He gave Baron a small, soft ball to squeeze, and after a few weeks, Baron's fingers got stronger so that he could write with his pencil for a longer time. Mr Tax also made sure that he stood close to Baron to explain his work to him.

After a while, Baron started to like doing his classwork. He started to listen to what Mr Tax had to say when he was teaching. Soon Baron was able to answer questions in class and help others with their worksheets.

Mr Tax was very pleased with Baron. One day he said, "Thank you for being willing to do your work. Because you were willing, you have done very well. Did you know that it is the Lord who wants you to do this work?"

"No, Mr Tax." Baron was surprised that the Lord would care about him doing schoolwork. "Why does the Lord want me to do my work?"

Mr Tax replied, "He wants you to do your work so that you get ready for whatever job he has for you to do when you grow up."

Baron was now even more willing to work, because now he was going to get ready for whatever the Lord wanted him to do when he grew up.

Mr Tax asked Baron to tell the class what he learnt about being willing.

Baron stood in front of the class and said, "I learnt that being willing means that I am to be happy to learn and do my work. I learnt that being willing helps me to do my work faster. And I learnt that if I am willing to do work, I have to pay attention to Mr Tax when he is teaching."

Baron turned to Mr Tax and said, "And, Mr Tax, I'm very glad that you were willing to help me."

Mr Tax smiled. "That's what I'm here for. I will always be willing to help each of you, and most importantly, the Lord will always be there to help you too."

2

Use Precious Materials

The materials willingly given to make the physical tabernacle were *precious* materials. *Precious* means "important, valuable, special."

The tabernacle, and all that was used to create it, was made out of *precious* materials. These materials included metals, fabrics, animal skins, wood, oils, and stones.

> And this is the offering which you shall take from them: gold, silver, and bronze; blue, purple, and scarlet thread, fine linen, and goats' hair; ram skins dyed red, badger skins, and acacia wood; oil for the light, and spices for the anointing oil and for the sweet incense; onyx stones, and stones to be set in the ephod and in the breastplate. (Exodus 25:3–7)

All those who would use or go into the tabernacle were to see these *precious* materials and remember that God is *precious* and holy.

Satan is the one who fights against God. He hates all that is good and true. All that is good and true is found only in God and with God. Anything that agrees with God and follows what God says is good and true. Who God is, what He thinks, what He likes, and what He wants can be seen in the Bible, or what we also call the Word of God.

For me to be a home for God, I must look like Him on the inside by having precious and holy thoughts and ways, just like Him. The *precious* materials that I must use to help build this type of holy place for God include the Word of God and prayer.

The Word of God is precious because it is a weapon against Satan. It can be like a sword or an arrow which attacks Satan whether he is far or near.

When Satan is far away, it means he is working outside me. For example, he might try to get other children at school to hurt me by saying mean things to me.

When Satan is near, it means he is working inside me. For example, he might give me bad thoughts about my brothers and sisters or try to get me to hate doing what is right, or he might attack my body to make me feel sick.

I can fight Satan when I use the Word of God because it hits him the way an arrow pierces its target, and like a sword it cuts through its target.

Satan is my target, and I fight him with the weapon called the Word of God. When I load this into my prayers, I can beat Satan up all the time.

Rafael's Giving Costs Something

Rafael held on to the money in his hand. Then he placed it in his underwear drawer to make sure he would always know where it was. Uncle Bob had given him this money so that he could pay to ride a horse at the upcoming fair.

After Rafael saw the movie *Black Beauty,* he fell in love with horses and longed to ride one. He spoke about it with great excitement whenever he had an opportunity. Rafael even dreamt about what it would feel like to ride a horse.

The day of the fair came, and while the rest of his family was trying to decide what to do first, Rafael was already heading towards the area where the horses were to be confined. When Rafael got to this spot he was disappointed to see that they had not arrived as yet. That didn't dampen his joy, though. Rafael had fun watching his friends and family on the slides and other rides.

Finally, Rafael turned round to see the horses being led to the riding area. They were more beautiful in real life than he had imagined. There were five horses: black, brown, grey and white, white with black spots all over, and brown with white. But the black one caught his eye the most. It reminded him of his favourite story, *Black Beauty.* So with one great leap of joy, Rafael ran over to the riding area as fast as he could. A line had already formed, but he did not mind waiting.

His best friend, Kirk, was there too. He stood on the side watching the caretakers put the horses in place for the next set of young riders. Rafael wondered why Kirk did not join the line. He asked the boy behind him to hold his spot and off he went to get Kirk.

"Hey, Kirk, come in the line with me."

"No, thanks. I don't like horses," Kirk said glumly.

"I thought you did," Rafael replied.

As Rafael stood in line he heard two boys from his school talking. One said to the other, "Did you hear that Kirk lost his wallet when he got here?"

Then Rafael realised that it wasn't the horses that Kirk did not like. It was that Kirk did not have any money to pay for a turn to ride one.

Rafael reached his hand into his pocket and pulled out the money his uncle Bob had given to him. "Here, Kirk, go ahead."

Kirk looked at his friend in disbelief. "This is a lot of money. You could go on a lot of different rides with this."

Rafael smiled. "Yeah, but you're my best friend. Go ahead."

Kirk's face brightened, and off he went to join the line. Rafael watched as his friend rode the black beauty. Then he felt a hand on his shoulder. When he looked up, it was Uncle Bob.

"I saw what you did. Riding a horse was precious to you, and you'd waited for it for so long, and yet you gave it up. Why?"

"Kirk's my best friend. He's more important to me than the horse ride."

Uncle Bob was amazed.

Rafael explained. "I was taught at church that if someone is precious or important, you're to always think of him or her first, look out for that person, and want what's best for them."

Uncle Bob grabbed Rafael's hand and shook it. When Uncle Bob took his hand away, Rafael felt something in his hand.

Rafael looked and in his hand was enough money for a horse ride. Rafael smiled brightly, thanked Uncle Bob, and ran off to join the line.

Riesa's Special Place

Riesa had several questions for her friend Tania as the two sat on the field eating lunch.

"Have you ever wondered why we were born?" Riesa asked.

Tania replied, "I don't know. I never really thought about it."

"Do you wonder what life will be like for you when you get older?" Riesa asked.

Tania shrugged. "No, not really." She bit into her ham sandwich with great gusto. As her mouth cleared, she grunted. "All I care about is cheerleading after school. I've been working on my double flip, and I'm going to show that Keri Sullins something that she'll never, ever forget."

Riesa could see that her friend did not care much about what she was asking. "What's more important than cheerleading, Tania? Do you even wonder if there really is a God?"

Tania rolled her eyes and made a face at her friend. "Why do you care?"

Riesa felt a little stupid for wanting to know about God. It seemed like her friends didn't care about those things.

Riesa kept quiet all the way to the store with Cousin Keith, who had met her after school.

Cousin Keith saw that Riesa was not very happy at all. "Why so glum?" he asked.

"I wanted to know who made me and what I was made to do, but I think my friends think I'm stupid."

Cousin Keith was a little shocked that Riesa was having such thoughts. He did not think children so young actually wanted to know about the One who created them.

Riesa glanced at Cousin Keith. "You think I'm stupid too, don't you?"

Cousin Keith replied, "Riesa, I don't think you're stupid, and I know where you can get your answers to those questions and everything you will ever face in your whole life."

Riesa spun around to look at Cousin Keith's face to see if he was being serious.

"It's true, Riesa. There is a place, a very special place, where you can learn about the Lord and see all that He wants for you to do in the earth. You can see all about what happened in the past and learn all about what is happening in the present and will happen in the future."

Riesa was thrilled. She could not wait to see such a place.

Cousin Keith said, "I'll show you after we leave the store. I promise."

When the two finally made it to Riesa's home, Cousin Keith went to the bookshelf in the study and came back with a book in his hand.

"A book!" Riesa said. "How can that be the place to tell me why I was born?"

Cousin Keith pointed and said, "It's no ordinary book. It's the Bible. It contains the Word of God, who is the Creator of heaven and Earth, the One who has all power, who knows the past, present, and future."

Riesa sat for a long time reading. Cousin Keith was amazed to see that she was happy to stay put for so long. Now and again Riesa asked him a question, and he was glad to answer.

Riesa was fascinated to learn about Abraham, Jacob, Joseph, Moses, and Daniel and to see how God talked to them and told them where to go and what to do. She saw that they knew God was real and that they believed in Him. The more she read, the more she learnt, and the more she learnt, the more she wanted to know God too.

A few days later, Cousin Keith came over, and Riesa's mum said, "What did you do to Riesa? She likes to carry that Bible everywhere she goes. It is now her favourite book."

Cousin Keith laughed. Then Riesa walked into the living room. Cousin Keith said, "I hear that you like reading the Bible."

Riesa replied, "You were right. It's no ordinary book. I think the Word of God is the most precious thing in the whole world."

3

Watch and Listen

Being willing and having precious materials were not all that the people needed. Those who built the physical tabernacle also needed to *watch* and *listen* to God so that they knew exactly how to use their skills and the precious materials He gave them.

This teaches me that I need to *watch* and *listen* to God so that I know how to think, say, and do all that is right to please Him. Two of the ways I can do this is to watch and listen to the people God has given to me.

I do some things without having to be taught, such as breathing and other things that happen inside my body. But there are lots and lots of things that I have to be shown how to do, such as how to read, write, tie my shoelaces, play football, or do gymnastics.

If I do not watch and listen to my mummy, daddy, and teachers, I will not know how to do the things they try to teach me. And if I listen only to part of what they say and not the whole thing, I will not know how to fully do what I am to do. I have to listen to everything God says if I want to be a good home for Him.

"And let them make Me a sanctuary, that I may dwell among them. According to all that I show you, that is, the pattern of the tabernacle and the pattern of all its furnishings, just so you shall make it." (Exodus 25:8–9)

Cali's Experiment

Samantha and her classmates each placed all the tools and materials they needed for the experiment on their desks. This included a potato, a Petri dish, chemicals, droppers, and a microscope.

Mr Snag walked around the class to make sure each student was ready. He said, "At the end of the class, you will be graded for your project. Watch and listen carefully to all that I say and do."

Everyone was quiet except for Cali Jones. Cali Jones was always the noisy one. Samantha was convinced that Cali did not know the meaning of the word "quiet".

Cali pulled her table so that it scraped along the floor and made a horrible screeching noise.

Mr Snag gave her a look.

"Oh, sorry, Mr Snag. I wanted to make sure I could see you better so I had to move my table."

Cali knew herself well. She could easily fall into daydreaming if given the opportunity. To her, the imaginary world was a lot more fun than the real one, especially when it came to subjects like science, which she found a bit boring.

But this time Cali planned to watch Mr Snag well so as not to miss anything. The rest of the class moaned and rolled their eyes, but Mr Snag continued as if nothing had happened.

Whatever Mr Snag did, the other students did too. He cut, and they cut. He used a certain chemical, and they used that chemical too. Finally, Mr Snag instructed the children each to place their piece of potato under the lens of their microscope.

Then the students had to write down everything they saw, did, and learnt.

Mr Snag did his usual walk around. When he got to Cali's desk, he didn't just pause—he stopped. "Cali Jones, come see me after class."

Class ended, and everyone left. Cali stood before Mr Snag.

Mr Snag rubbed his forehead as if to somehow comfort himself before he began. "Cali, you are the only one who has a different result for your experiment. Everyone else had a green result, but you had an orange result. Did you follow my instructions carefully?"

"Yes, Mr Snag. I had all the right materials and tools, and I watched everything you did."

Mr Snag looked at Cali. "Did you *listen* to all that I said?"

Cali shifted from one leg to the next. "I tried to, but sometimes I start thinking about other things, like the new bicycle I got for my birthday yesterday. It has ten gears and I can't wait to try them all out. Plus, I'm spending the weekend with my aunt. I can't wait!"

Mr Snag rubbed his forehead again and sighed. "Cali, if you only watched what I was doing but were not listening all the time, you were not paying careful attention. That means you would not have heard when I said to put in four drops of one chemical and two of the other."

Cali said, "I'm sorry, sir. I thought watching was enough."

Mr Snag turned Cali's paper around so that she could see the mark.

Cali sighed. "Next time I'll listen too."

Mr Snag responded, "Yes, Cali. In order to understand something completely, you have to watch what is going on and also listen to what is being said. If you practise this, you will get better grades, OK?"

Cali smiled and replied, "Yes, sir."

Nate's Promise

Nate sat under the tree to eat his sandwich and snack. It was peaceful here, and he preferred it to being in the canteen or pacing up and down the school corridors with his peers constantly babbling and yelling.

Nate liked to listen to the birds making their calls to one another and to watch them fuss over the little hatchlings in their nests.

It reminded him of how parents fuss over their "little hatchlings" on the first day of school and of how his mum had fussed over him. She tucked in his shirt and looked inside his bag several times to make sure he had his favourite colouring book, crayons, and cap. Although Nate was very young, he saw that his mum was really nervous about him going to school for the first time. She had asked him if he was OK more times than she usually did.

It was a memory he never wanted to forget, because shortly after school began, his mum had been in a car accident and died. He missed hearing her voice and seeing her flitter around getting his lunch and packing his bag for school. And he remembered how she read the Bible to him at night and how she told him that he must watch and listen to God.

Once Nate had asked, "Mum, how can I watch God?"

She had replied by pinching his nose playfully and giving him a light tickle on his tummy. Then she said, "You can watch God in two ways. You can look in the Bible and read about all that He said and did. As for the second way, you can watch those who believe in God. They are to be your living examples of what a godly person is like."

Nate had rested his head on her lap and asked, "How can I listen to God?"

His mum stroked his head and said, "Listening is more than just hearing something. You have to pay attention to it and let it change the way you think and behave."

Nate remembered how she had laughed when she looked down and saw the blank stare on his face.

"For example," she continued, "you must do more than just look at the Word of God—you must listen to it. The words in the Bible have a voice, and when you read them, they speak to you on the inside of your spirit and soul.

"I remember when I read about Esther and the golden sceptre. Esther prayed and sought God and then bravely went before the king. That could have resulted in her death, but because she trusted God, the king held out his sceptre and she went to him. As I read that, I saw how I had to trust God and be obedient and brave. Those words that I read spoke to me and help me every day."

Nate remembered how deep and thoughtful her eyes were as she spoke those words. Then, looking at him, she had said, "Nate, there is One you must get to know and have a relationship with all your life. He will teach you what the scriptures mean, and He will give you the strength to do what is right. He is God the Holy Spirit."

Nate promised that he would get to know God, and the two cuddled that night for the last time. Nate never forgot what she said. And as Nate walked back to his class, he clutched the Bible his mum had given him and said, "Lord, help me watch and listen to You always."

4

Go through the Gate

The physical tabernacle was built and set up exactly in the way God wanted. It was surrounded by a fence so that you could not get in without going through the gate. A *gate* is an opening or way of getting into a property or place. The surrounding wall, with no other opening, lets you know that you cannot get into the property except by using the gate.

This teaches me about Jesus, who said: "I am the door. If anyone enters by me, he will be saved" (John 10:9), and "I am the way, the truth, and the life. No one comes to the Father except through me" (John 14:6).

The gate and all that happened inside the physical tabernacle helps me see who Jesus is and why I need Him. Just as I need to *go through* a physical gate to get into a property, I need to go through the spiritual gate called Jesus to enter into heaven.

I go through Jesus because I see that material things can't help me know what is right from wrong. Material things—such as tablets, laptops, books, and clothing may be helpful tools, but they do not have the truth in them that can save me from Satan.

I go through Jesus because I see the bad things that happen all around me.

I go through Jesus because I see that I have bad thoughts and ways inside me. Satan can put thoughts in me to be selfish and to hate correction, schoolwork, parents, teachers, tidying up, and even everything God says. If I listen to those thoughts and hate those good things, I will do what Satan wants me to do.

I go through Jesus because I see that He is the only one who can save *all* of me—spirit, soul, and body.

I go through Jesus because He is the only One who can help me to do what is right all the time. Satan hates all that God has created: the heavens, the earth, and all that is in them, especially me. He wants me to be just like him. The only one who can save me from being like Satan is Jesus.

Boys on the Prowl

Tim had heard that the newly built house in the next neighbourhood was being outfitted with slides, swings, and a large pool. For weeks his friends went on about how they could not wait to go on the slides.

Tim asked them, "How are you going to get to go on the slides and the swings? Isn't there a fence?"

His friends convinced him there was no wall or gate.

So one day, Tim and six friends decided to go down to this house. They talked about how they were going to swing and slide and then go for a swim in the pool.

But when they got there, it was not what they expected. There was a huge wall, so that they could not even see into the garden. It was clear that they would not be able to climb over the wall.

They walked around the property and saw that there was indeed no way to get into the property except through the gate. And the gate was high, so they could not climb over it, either. The boys were disappointed and a bit upset that they were not able to get the joyous time they wanted.

When they returned to Tim's house, they told Uncle Joe about the adventure they'd had and how they did not get to see the things behind the wall.

Uncle Joe shook his head disapprovingly at the boys. "Why did you think you could just go on someone else's property without permission? Didn't you think it belonged to someone, and the person would invite who they wanted to come in?"

The boys were taken aback and ashamed.

Uncle Joe continued, "The one who is invited is the one who gets to go through the gate, which is the right way in. That person would not even think about climbing the wall. Only thieves and evil men try to get into a place and take or use things that do not belong to them."

Tim and his friends apologised.

The next time the boys went by the grand house, they saw a boy who was about to go in through the gate. The boy looked back at them and said, "Would you like to come in and play with me on the slides and swings?"

Tim and his friends looked at one another and quickly joined the boy. Now the boys understood more about what Uncle Joe had been saying. They felt good to be going through the gate because it was the right way to enter the property. Never again did they think about trying to get in another way.

Janise Sees Herself

Janise was learning why people go through Jesus and why she should too. The first thing she learnt was that she should go through Jesus because of all the bad things she saw happening in the world around her.

After learning that, Janise watched the way other people behave. She saw children boasting, or fighting with words and objects. She saw children who did not like to share or get corrected by parents or teachers. Janise was glad she did not behave like those other children.

One Saturday, Janise's dad took her to the fair. She had a good time riding on the merry-go-round and the ponies. Her dad bought her favourite treats: cotton candy, ice cream, and pizza. Janise was very happy inside, and it showed on the outside. She could not stop smiling and skipping as she followed her dad to the next fun tent.

Then Dad's cellular phone rang, and Janise could tell he was very upset. Dad replied to the caller, "Thank you for calling, Coach. I'm on my way."

Janise did not understand what was happening. Her dad grabbed her arm and hurried her to their car. In the car, Mr Gwen told Janise that her older sister, Kezzy, had fallen while playing lawn tennis and might have broken her arm.

As Dad drove quickly along the streets, Janise felt sorry that Kezzy was hurt, but she could not stop thinking about all the fun rides she was yet to go on. She could not stop thinking about Dad's promise to win her a big blue stuffed bear. Janise became more than upset—she was just plain angry.

When they reached the hospital, there was Kezzy with tears streaming down her face and a cast woven around her arm. Mr Gwen put his arms around Kezzy to comfort her, and she rested her head on their dad's broad shoulders. He wiped her tears away and told her it was going to be OK. It wasn't long before Mr Gwen got his daughter to smile again. The coach said her goodbyes and off she went.

Mr Gwen noticed that Janise had curled up in a chair and did not come over to say hello to her sister or ask if she was OK. "Janise, are you all right?" he asked.

"No!" Janise replied sharply.

"What's wrong? Why are you so angry?" Dad asked.

"I wanted to stay at the fair, and you promised me that you would get me a big blue bear."

"I know, Janise, but your sister needed me. And isn't she more important than the big blue bear?"

Janise did not say anything.

"Aren't you even going to give your big sis a hug?" Dad pleaded.

"No. This is all her fault." Now Janise was being very rude. "She should have been careful when she was playing. She messed up my good time."

Kezzy got off the examination bed, came over to her little sister, and asked, "Jan, do you remember why people go through Jesus to be saved?"

"Yes, they go through Jesus because of the bad things they see happening around them."

"Correct, Jan. But that's only one reason. They also go through Jesus because of the bad things they see happening inside them."

"What do you mean?" Janise asked.

"You can see the bad things around you, but you are not seeing the bad things that are happening inside you too. Satan puts thoughts inside you, and you can choose to listen to them or not. Right now you are angry with me because I got hurt. Don't you care about me?"

Janise loved her sister and did not want anything bad to happen to her. She knew then that these thoughts of hate and feelings of anger must have come from Satan. She had listened to him and let fun at the fair become more important than her sister.

"I'm sorry, Kezzy. I can see that I am not good on the inside. What am I going to do?"

Kezzy took her little sister's hand and kissed it. "Go through Jesus, who is the only one who can help us do what is right all the time."

5

Make Acceptable Sacrifices

Sacrifices were made in the physical tabernacle. During the time when the tabernacle was set up, the Israelites sacrificed animals such as cattle, goats, and sheep.

> Now the LORD spoke to Moses, saying, "Speak to the children of Israel, saying: 'If a person sins unintentionally against any of the commandments of the LORD in anything which ought not to be done, and does any of them, if the anointed priest sins, bringing guilt on the people, then let him offer to the LORD for his sin which he has sinned a young bull without blemish as a sin offering. He shall bring the bull to the door of the tabernacle of meeting before the LORD, lay his hand on the bull's head, and kill the bull before the LORD." (Leviticus 4:1–4)

A *sacrifice* is something I have that I give up or give away. It can be a physical thing, such as clothes, food, and toys, or it can be something not physical, such as time.

When I sacrifice or give up a physical thing such as food, I give some or all away to someone else instead of eating it all myself.

When I sacrifice something that is not physical, such as time, I take the time I have to do what I want, such as playing or watching a movie, and instead use that time to help someone else.

God said that whatever the sacrifice or offering is, it has to be something that is *acceptable* to Him. *Acceptable* means that something is pleasing to the Lord.

How can I make my sacrifices acceptable or pleasing to the Lord?

- **Do or give willingly.** I do not grumble and complain when I do or give something.
- **Do or give my best.** When the Israelites tried to sacrifice animals that were sick or injured, the Lord did not like that they wanted to keep the best for themselves and cared more about their possessions than about God.

> And when you offer the blind as a sacrifice, Is it not evil? And when you offer the lame and sick, Is it not evil? Offer it then to your governor! Would he be pleased with you? Would he accept you favorably?" Says the LORD of hosts. (Malachi 1:8)

- **Do or give in obedience.** To be obedient is to listen and do the good that I am told to do.

> And Saul said to Samuel, "But I have obeyed the voice of the LORD, and gone on the mission on which the LORD sent me, and brought back Agag, king of Amalek; I have

utterly destroyed the Amalekites. But the people took of the plunder, sheep and oxen, the best of the things which should have been utterly destroyed, to sacrifice to the Lᴏʀᴅ your God in Gilgal." So Samuel said: "Has the Lᴏʀᴅ as great delight in burnt offerings and sacrifices, as in obeying the voice of the Lᴏʀᴅ? Behold, to obey is better than sacrifice, And to heed than the fat of rams." (1 Samuel 15:20–22)

I have learnt that I should be careful to do what the Lord asks without making up excuses for doing the opposite and being disobedient, because God always knows the real reason for what I say and do.

Give Your Best

Mrs Lent sat teaching her two boys, Thomas and Ben, about what makes a sacrifice acceptable to the Lord.

"Do you remember what a sacrifice is?" Mrs Lent asked.

"Yes, Mummy," the boys answered together.

"What is it, Thomas?"

"A sacrifice is when you give someone something that is important to you."

Then Ben's hand shot up in the air to get his mummy's attention.

"Yes, Ben, what do you think a sacrifice is?"

"It is when you take the time to do something for someone even though you could be doing something else you like doing, like watching television."

"Very good, boys; you are both correct. I'm very glad to see that you have been listening to what I have been saying. Which one of you will be the first to tell me what the word acceptable means?"

Both Thomas and Ben's arms were raised, and Mummy could not decide whom to call on first. So she wrote down both names, threw them in a bag, and tossed them around before pulling out one.

"OK, Thomas, tell me what acceptable means."

"It means that something is pleasing to the Lord so that He accepts or takes it from you."

"Can I add too?" Ben asked.

"Go ahead," Mummy said.

"For the things we do to be acceptable, we have to do them willingly," he said with a wide grin.

Mummy, Thomas, and Ben then heard the alarm go off, and that meant Bible study time was over.

"Oh no!" the boys cried.

They liked Bible study very much but did not like what came next. It was time to do chores.

Before they began, Mummy explained to the boys that chores were a good way to practice giving acceptable sacrifices. She said that although the boys could spend their time doing other things, they needed to learn to give thought, time, and energy to things which are a help to their family.

Mummy asked, "Do you remember who is doing what today?"

"Yes," Thomas said, "I'm washing the dishes and bathing the dogs today."

"And what about you, Ben?" Mummy asked.

"I'm neatly packing away books and toys."

"Off you go then," she said.

The two boys ran off in different directions. Thomas ran outside, and Ben ran to their bedroom. After some time had passed, Mummy saw the boys playing in the yard.

"Have you both finished your chores?" she asked.

Both boys yelled, "Yes, Mummy!"

Then Mummy went to the bedroom. Ben had packed all the toys away neatly, but the books were still on the floor. Then Mummy went outside to check on the dogs. They had been bathed and dried. Mummy checked the kitchen sink. The dishes were all washed, but when she looked closer, she saw that two of the plates and some of the forks still had bits of food on them.

Mummy called the boys to her. "Ben, why didn't you put the books on the shelf?"

"I was tired," Ben said.

"Not too tired to play, though," Mummy said angrily. "And what about you, Thomas? Why didn't you make sure that you washed the dishes properly?"

Thomas' gaze dropped to the floor.

Mummy's face told the boys that she was not pleased with them. "Is your sacrifice acceptable?" she asked.

"Not all of it, Mummy," Thomas and Ben said together.

Thomas spoke first. "My sacrifice of bathing the dogs was acceptable because I did it willingly, but my sacrifice of washing the dishes wasn't acceptable because I did not take the time to do it properly. I rushed through because I wanted to play outside with Ben."

Then Ben spoke. "My sacrifice of packing away the toys was *acceptable* because I was happy to do it, but I didn't want to pack away the books so I did a bad job."

"Was this the best that you could do?" Mummy asked.

Both boys shook their heads.

"So what are you going to do?" she asked.

Thomas ran to the kitchen, and Ben ran to their bedroom. When Mummy checked later, the books were neatly in place and the dishes were scrubbed clean.

Later, Mummy asked the boys what else they had learnt about making a sacrifice acceptable to the Lord.

Together they chimed, "It must be the best that we can give."

Give in Obedience

Pat liked to sacrifice or give to others by helping them, but she could not understand why her help was often not met with pleasing looks or warm smiles.

Mother passed and saw Pat slouching on the couch with her arms folded and looking very deep in thought, almost as if she was daydreaming.

"What's wrong?" Mother asked.

"No one likes it when I try to help them. No one likes my sacrifices," Pat replied.

"That's not true," Mother said. She was a bit surprised to hear Pat say such a thing.

Pat pouted. "It is true. Today I tried to help you tidy up by picking up all my things from my bedroom floor, but you were angry with me."

"Pat, I wasn't angry with you for trying to pick up your things from the bedroom floor. I was angry because you were told to pick up your things since yesterday and you did not do it. Because you were not obedient, I had to change my plans for this morning."

Pat remembered then that her mother had asked her to tidy her room, but she had been reading her favourite book and did not want to stop. So she decided to do it later, even though Mother had asked for it to be done at that time.

"I'm sorry, Mother."

"I know, Pat. It's a good thing to give a sacrifice of tidying up, but it would be really helpful if you listened and did it when I asked you to do it."

"I understand. But what about when I tried to help Dad by tidying up his tools for him? That was helpful, but Dad was angry too."

Mother looked at Pat. "What does Dad always tell you about his tools?"

Pat thought about it. "Dad always says that he has his tools set out in the way he likes them so that he can find the one he wants easily when he needs it. But it looked so messy that I thought he would be happier with a tidier workshop."

"Yes, I know you thought it looked messy, but Dad told you he liked it that way. So why do you think Dad was not pleased when you packed all his tools away so neatly?"

Pat began to see that her sacrifice, or the time she gave to pack away her dad's tools, was not acceptable or pleasing because she had been disobedient.

"I think it's because I did not listen to Dad. I only did what I thought would be a good thing without thinking about what he wanted." Pat looked sad. "So how am I going to be able to give sacrifices that are acceptable to the Lord?"

Mother hugged Pat. "Well, from what we have discussed, what do you think is the problem?"

"Umm … the things I did were good because tidying up is a good thing, but it was not acceptable or pleasing because I was disobedient."

The next day, when Mother asked Pat to tidy her room, she put away her favourite book and did as she was asked. And when Mother saw the tidy room, she was pleased. Then Pat knew her sacrifice was acceptable because she had listened and did what she was asked to do in the right time.

6

Answer the Call

The priests in the tabernacle were separated from others in order to serve God and God's people. Before the priests were able to work in the tabernacle, they had to be *called*, washed, and dressed.

> And Aaron and his sons you shall bring to the door of the tabernacle of meeting, and you shall wash them with water. Then you shall take the garments, put the tunic on Aaron, and the robe of the ephod, the ephod, and the breastplate, and gird him with the intricately woven band of the ephod. You shall put the turban on his head, and put the holy crown on the turban. And you shall take the anointing oil, pour it on his head, and anoint him. Then you shall bring his sons and put tunics on them. And you shall gird them with sashes, Aaron and his sons, and put the hats on them. The priesthood shall be theirs for a perpetual statute. So you shall consecrate Aaron and his sons. (Exodus 29:4–9)

To be *called* means I am given *authority* and *ability* from God to do the job that He has called or given me to do.

To have *authority* means I have been given the right to say and do certain things. The priests were given the right by God to say and do all that He told them to say and do.

To have *ability* is to have what I need to get the job done—for example, tools, materials, talent, information, and understanding.

God has called me to serve Him and His people, and this means He will give me everything I need to do this well.

> So you [Moses] shall speak to all who are gifted artisans, whom I have filled with the spirit of wisdom, that they may make Aaron's garments, to consecrate him, that he may minister to me as priest. (Exodus 28:3)

As I grow, I learn more about the kinds of things I have the right to say and do. I learn these things from those God has given to me, such as my parents, teachers, pastors, and the Holy Spirit.

I also learn about what kinds of talents I have, such as singing, dancing, or drawing, and I learn what tools I will need to use with those talents to do what God has called me to do.

For example, if God calls me to be a singer, then I will find that I have a love for music and singing. My parents and teachers can help me learn notes and pitches. And the Holy Spirit will help me know exactly how to use music and singing to teach others about Jesus.

> And Moses said to the children of Israel, "See, the LORD has called by name Bezalel the son of Uri, the son of Hur, of the tribe of Judah; and He has filled him with the Spirit of God, in wisdom and understanding, in knowledge and all manner of workmanship, to design artistic works, to work in gold and silver and bronze, in cutting jewels for setting, in carving wood, and to work in all manner of artistic workmanship." And He has put in his heart

the ability to teach, in him and Aholiab the son of Ahisamach, of the tribe of Dan. (Exodus 35:30–34)

Collin's Authority

It was the beginning of a new school year, the time when the class prefect was named. The teacher was the one who chose this person, who had to make sure all the other children kept the classroom clean by picking up trash and placing it in the garbage bin. The prefect also had to make sure the chairs and desks were left tidy after school and that the children kept quiet when the teacher was not there.

Being a prefect was not an easy job because the prefect also had to take any classmate who did not listen to the principal's office. The prefect had to do this even if the classmate was a friend. This did not make the prefect well liked at all, but it was part of the job.

Mr Grant stood in front of the class. "OK, class, I have the name of the new prefect."

Everyone was silent. They sat on the edge of their seats and waited. Although it was not an easy job to be called to do, anyone chosen was glad to be called because it meant the teacher trusted that student as a person who was honest, kind, fair, and obedient. It was an honour to be class prefect.

Mr Grant broke the suspense. "Collin, please come up."

All the students clapped, and Collin's face lit up as he approached Mr Grant. He was pleased to be called to be a prefect. He had learnt at church that he was to do everything to please the Lord, and he wanted very much to please the Lord by being a good prefect.

Mr Grant pinned the badge on Collin's shirt, and Collin stood proud before the class.

The next day, Collin was forced to speak to a boy from another class who had eaten his snack and thrown the wrapper down in the pathway.

"Jermaine, stop right there. You need to pick up that wrapper and put it in the bin."

Jermaine turned around, stuck out his tongue at Collin, and said, "What gives you the right to tell me what to do?"

Collin pointed to his badge. "My teacher did."

Jermaine stuck his tongue out again and turned to walk away, only to bump straight into Mr Grant, who looked at him sternly.

"Jermaine, Collin has my permission and the permission of all the teachers and the principal to tell you what to do, and you are to listen to him. That is what his badge means. He was called to do a job, and you are to do what he says."

Jermaine was embarrassed and turned to Collin. "Sorry for the way I spoke to you."

Collin nodded. Jermaine picked up his wrapper and threw it into the bin.

That day Jermaine learnt that the prefect was called to do a job by someone higher than himself, like the teachers and principal of the school, and that meant Collin had the right or the permission to tell him what to do.

When Collin got home, he thought about how being called to be a prefect was like being called to be a priest. A priest is also called. He is called by God and given permission to tell others what God would have them do.

Collin thanked God for calling him to serve his classmates and teachers. He thanked God for the authority He gave him to do this. Collin also asked God to help him to use this authority in the right way.

🐾 Alice's Ability

Alice stretched across her bed and looked up at the shelf which housed all her craft pieces. She had won prizes for many of her pieces, but some were her favourites. She especially liked the boat, the horse, the car, and the helicopter. Nevertheless, she had enjoyed making all of them.

Suddenly, Dad's voice broke through her thoughts as he called out her name.

"Yes, Dad! I'm coming!"

Off she ran. She found her dad sitting in the living room with company.

"Allie, your Uncle Rae and Cousin Paul are here because they need your help."

Alice turned to look at her uncle and cousin. She could not believe these men would need her help, and the puzzled look on her face gave that away.

"Yes," Cousin Paul said, "you can help us. We want to show our new clients a model or example of how the new restaurant we want to build for them will look. We have a picture here for you to look at."

Cousin Paul pointed to Uncle Rae, who pulled out a long, rolled-up sheet of card from behind him. When he spread it out on the table, Alice saw a picture of a restaurant with tables, chairs, and a water fountain next to a car park.

"Wow!" Alice's eyes opened wide. "You want me to put this all into a craft model?"

Uncle Rae and Cousin Paul laughed. "Do you think you will be able to do something like that?"

"Oh yes, I can!" cried Alice excitedly. "The Lord has given me the talent of putting things together. I can already see in my mind exactly how I will get this done. It will be my biggest craft project ever!"

The men looked at each other with big smiles on their faces. They were glad to see that Alice was excited to do this, but most of all they were pleased to see that Alice knew that her ability to do these things was given to her by the Lord.

Alice stood up and scratched her head. "But if I am going to be able to do this, I will need some materials. I will need lots of craft sticks, glue, paint, and card."

Cousin Paul smiled. He reached over the side of the couch and pulled up a large bag. "Here you go. We knew that for you to be able to do this, you would need these."

Alice jumped for joy. She could not wait to get started. She hugged her uncle and cousin. "Thank you, thank you."

Uncle Rae chuckled, and then his expression changed. He looked at Alice with a serious face. "You were right, Allie, when you said the Lord has given you this talent or way of understanding and getting these things done. We are not able to do this, so we are thankful that you are willing to use your ability to help us."

That afternoon, before Alice started putting the project together, she prayed. "Thank you, Lord, for giving me the ability to put craft pieces together. I know that it's You who always gives me the ideas, the understanding, the energy, and the strength to do everything. And I know that it is You, Lord, who also makes me willing to do it. Thank you for making me able to do this. You not only gave me the talent, you also gave me the materials and tools that I need to do this job. Help me do a good job for my uncle and cousin. Amen."

7

Get Washed

After the priests were called, they were *washed*.

> And Aaron and his sons you shall bring to the door
> of the tabernacle of meeting, and you shall wash
> them with water. (Exodus 29:4)

This shows me that it is important to be made clean before you work for God.

Like the tabernacle priests, I *wash* my body so that I remove dirt and germs and get clean. This is something that I have to do all the time. If I do not wash my body properly, I can get sick or very itchy and smelly. I can also make clean things dirty when I touch them with my dirty hands.

It is good to be clean on the outside, but more importantly, God wants me to be clean on the inside as well.

> Now may the God of peace Himself sanctify you
> completely; and may your whole spirit, soul, and
> body be preserved blameless at the coming of our
> Lord Jesus Christ. (1 Thessalonians 5:23)

The inside of me is my spiritual part that is unseen, and the outside of me is my physical part that can be seen. My spiritual part is made up of my spirit and soul. My physical part is made up of all my physical body parts. Both these parts are joined to make up the whole of me.

My spirit is what I use to communicate with God. It is like a phone. I can call out to God, and He can call in to me.

My mind, will, intellect, and emotions are in my soul. My soul is the place where I have thoughts and memories and desires to do or have something. It is also where I learn and store information from all that I see and hear at school and anywhere I go, such as how to read, do mathematics, or play sports and instruments. It is also the place where I feel happiness, sadness, anger, peace, anxiousness, and other emotions.

This poem helps me to understand my spiritual or unseen part.

The Whole of Me Belongs to God

I have a spirit.
I have a soul.
I have a body.
All my parts make up
The whole of me,
The whole of me.

With my spirit I can hear God speak
Any time, in every day of the week.
I can tell God anything,
And He will answer all I bring.

I have a spirit.
I have a soul.
I have a body.
All my parts make up
The whole of me,
The whole of me.

My mind is in my soul.
With my mind I remember and think
About what happens throughout my days,
All my words and all my ways.

I have a spirit.
I have a soul.
I have a body.
All my parts make up
The whole of me,
The whole of me.

My will is in my soul.
With my will, I want to do or not do.
Here I say yes or no as I choose.
Here I win, or here I lose.

I have a spirit.
I have a soul.
I have a body.
All my parts make up
The whole of me,
The whole of me.

My intellect is in my soul.
My intellect is what I know,
The things I learn from what I hear and see
And my talents that make something easy for me.

I have a spirit.
I have a soul.
I have a body.
All my parts make up
The whole of me,
The whole of me.

My emotions are in my soul.
My emotions are the ways I feel,
Like being angry, scared, or sad
Or being excited or glad.

I have a spirit.
I have a soul.
I have a body.
All my parts make up
The whole of me,
The whole of me.

I have a physical body.
It has many parts to help me move and do.
With it I can watch, I can read, I can run, I can sing,
And I can lift a light or heavy thing.

I have a spirit.
I have a soul.
I have a body.
All my parts make up
The whole of me.
The whole of me.

The whole of me belongs to God.
He wants me to use all of my parts
To watch, listen, speak and do
All that is good and true.

Why do I need to wash the inside of me? Because it gets dirty from the bad or sinful things I think, say, and do. Things are bad or sinful when they are opposite to or go against what God says— for example, when I lie, steal, grumble, complain, or am rude or disobedient to the good I am told to do.

"For though you wash yourself with lye, and use much soap, yet your iniquity is marked before me" says the Lord God. (Jeremiah 2:22).

How can I wash the inside of me?

When I wash my outer physical body, I may use a washcloth, bath soap, and water. I also use different things to clean different parts of my body. I use shampoo for my hair and toothpaste for my teeth.

I cannot use bath soap, water from the tap, shampoo, or toothpaste to clean my spirit and soul. I need something that can go inside me and take away my dirty thoughts, ways, and attitudes. Only the Word of God can do that.

If I only looked at the bath soap and water but did not get into the shower to use it, I would stay dirty on the outside. If I only read the Word of God but do not believe it is true and that I need to change to match what God says, then I will stay dirty on the inside.

How can a young man cleanse his way? By taking heed according to Your word. With my whole heart I have sought You; oh, let me not wander from Your commandments! Your word I have hidden in my heart, that I might not sin against You. (Psalm 119: 9–11)

This psalm teaches me that I need to read, hear, know, believe, and live the Word of God so that I can stay clean on the inside after going to Jesus, who takes away all my sins.

Dirty Dan

Dan enjoyed playing outdoors. He and his friends dug in the dirt to find earthworms and snails. Then they pitched marbles on the lawn. Afterwards, they had races around the neighbourhood.

Jason was in charge of the stopwatch, and he wrote down how long it took each person to run around the block. After the five boys finished the course, the winner of the races was announced. Dan had the fastest time.

The boys laughed, and some put blades of grass on Dan's hair as a crown, bowing before him and saying, "You are the king of speed."

While Dan was out playing, Mum and Dad cleaned the home. They swept and mopped, changed the sheets on the beds, did the laundry, and scrubbed the sinks and toilets. After all the cleaning was done, they prepared dinner together. Dan's mum worked on the vegetables while his dad cooked the chicken and worked on the macaroni pie.

When Dan entered the house, he smelled the dinner, and the noisy rumble-tumble of his stomach gave away how hungry he was after a good afternoon of play.

Dan found his parents in the kitchen. "Hey, I'm back."

"Did you have fun?" Mum asked without actually turning to look at Dan.

"Yeah, I won the race around the neighbourhood."

Then Dad said, "You can't sit here like that!"

It was Dad's tone that made Mum turn to look at Dan. "Yikes!" she said. "You do look a horrible mess, and Dad's right, there's no way you are sitting for dinner like that. Go and *wash* everywhere, including your hair."

"Besides," Dad said with a grin, "your smell might make the dinner run off."

Mum and Dad both laughed, and so did Dan, who could picture the food with legs running away and screaming for help.

"All right, I'm going." And off Dan went to the bathroom to clean up.

He never liked bathing that much. It always seemed to take too long. First you had to take off all your clothes, wait for the water to get warm, get the washcloth all soapy, and remember all the body parts to wash. And if that wasn't enough of a time-waster, Dan now had the added joy of having to wash his hair, which meant rubbing in shampoo and washing it out twice. After all that, he would have to dry off, find clothes to wear, and get dressed.

As Dan stood there waiting for the water to get warm, he wondered why his parents didn't know that he had better things to do with his time. Maybe he could have handled it once a day, but it had to be done twice, once in the morning and once in the evening. Dan was not happy at all.

Suddenly, he had a brilliant idea. "I will throw a bit of water on my hair, wash my face and my hands, and just change my clothes. Then I will spray some of Dad's cologne on my clean shirt. That will make things quicker, and Mum and Dad will never know the difference. This will also mean that I can get a chance to play my favourite Nintendo game and still be ready to eat when dinner is ready."

And that was just what he did. Dan had a good time playing his Nintendo game, and when dinnertime was called, he rushed to his seat.

Mum and Dad recognised the strong cologne smell right away. "Did you bathe in water or in my cologne?" Dad asked.

Dan smiled. "I think I pressed out too much again. I won't use as much next time."

As they were eating, Mum paused and asked Dan, "Are you sure that you washed yourself properly?"

"Of course I did. I know how to wash myself properly, Mum."

Dan then started talking about the upcoming concert. Mum and Dad were happy to talk about the concert because Dan was going to be playing piano.

Later, when all was still and Dan should have been fast asleep, he woke up and started to scratch his arms, legs, back, and then his head and chest. It was irritating. Dan was itchy all over, and now he could not sleep.

Dan crept into his parents' room, tapped his mum, and whispered, "I can't sleep. I can't stop scratching, and my skin hurts."

Mum got up, wiped the sleep from her eyes, and went with Dan to his room. When she turned on the light to check his bed, the clean sheets looked dirty.

Mum turned to Dan. "You did not take a shower, did you?"

His expression was enough of an answer, and Dan knew exactly what he had to do. He went straight into the shower, shampooed, soaped up, and scrubbed clean. Afterwards, he returned to his room to find that his mum had placed a set of clean sheets on his bed.

When morning came, Dan went straight to his mum and dad. "I'm sorry for lying to you and for making the clean sheets dirty. I now see that when I am dirty, I make things around me dirty too. Besides that, it's really horrible being so itchy."

Dirty Maggie

Maggie's eyes opened wide as she watched the movie. She couldn't really tell who the good guys or the bad ones were. It seemed the good guys also did some bad things too, but that was no big deal to Maggie. She enjoyed the punches, kicks, and scuffling around which made for very entertaining fight scenes. Maggie found herself jumping and clapping with every blow dealt.

After the movie, Maggie listened to songs playing from the local radio station while she got ready to go out with her aunty

Sam. She recognised some of the songs because her friends sang them at school.

Maggie took a shower and got dressed. She did not realise that with every song, she started to feel angry on the inside. Some of the songs were about people who hated those who did not let them do what they wanted. And some of the songs were about how sad life was if you didn't have things like friends, cars, or the latest clothing. And others were about how you can't trust people. All the time the music was playing, Maggie was singing along and thinking that it was all so true.

Then the telephone rang as Maggie was about to put on her socks and shoes. It was Mother checking in. "Maggie, it's me. Did your aunty Sam get there as yet?"

Maggie replied, "Not yet, Mummy."

"Did you finish your homework and stay off that television like I asked you to?"

Maggie rolled her eyes impatiently. "Yes, Mummy, I did."

Then there was a sound of a car horn. "Mummy, I have to go. Aunty Sam is here," Maggie said.

Aunty Sam was Maggie's favourite aunt because she was honest and kind and always made Maggie laugh.

Aunty Sam thought it would be a good idea for the two of them to finish shopping for Maggie's school supplies before having lunch.

Maggie agreed, but as they walked around looking for school shoes and sneakers, Maggie found that she was getting really tired of Aunty Sam telling her that all the shoes she really liked were too expensive. In the end they agreed on the pairs of shoes that she needed, but Aunty Sam could see that Maggie was really not happy with them.

After that, Maggie spent the rest of time answering her aunt by shrugging her shoulders or shaking her head but never by speaking to her.

Aunty Sam stopped. "I think we need to go to lunch now."

As they sat, Aunty Sam said, "Maggie, we need to talk. What is bothering you so much that you are behaving like this?"

"I never get to do what I want or get what I want!" Maggie stated angrily.

"You've never behaved like this before. You've always understood that we don't have the money to do everything we want or get everything we want. You know that even if we had the money to get certain things, we still would not get them because we cannot frivolously spend what God has given us. You're acting like the shoes and other things we bought are not nice things too."

Maggie shrugged her shoulders and rolled her eyes.

"Maggie, you are not clean," Aunty Sam said.

Maggie inspected her clothing and then looked at her aunt. "Yes, I am. I showered and put on clean clothes."

"Yes, you're clean on the outside—but not on the inside."

"What do you mean?" Maggie asked.

"Well, you're being angry and rude, and that means you are not clean on the inside. You've put things into your spirit and soul that are dirty."

Maggie immediately knew what she had done wrong. She had

been watching violent movies and listening to music that made her feel angry and hate what she had.

Maggie held her head down and said, "It's true. I spent this whole morning filling my spirit and soul up with bad things. How can I get clean now?"

Aunty Sam looked Maggie in the eyes. "You can begin by saying sorry to the Lord, and you can tell the Lord about all the unclean things you have put inside yourself and ask Him to get rid of them."

Maggie agreed, and then she asked another question. "How can I stay clean on the inside?"

Aunty Sam sipped her hot tea and then said, "You see, Maggie, your life has to match the scriptures. Your life has to become the same as what the scriptures say. For example, the Word of God says you are not to lie, so that means you are to practise honesty. If you do this, you will be clean inside."

Maggie knew her aunt was telling the truth because she was a very honest person. Maggie apologised to the Lord and to her aunt. She also promised to do the same with her mother later that day.

Aunty Sam prayed with Maggie, and after lunch the two had a very enjoyable afternoon. Maggie learnt that there are things that make you dirty on the inside and that it is important to get washed by saying sorry and living to match the scriptures.

8

Get Dressed

After the priests were called and washed, they got *dressed*. God told them exactly how they were to *dress* so that their private parts and the rest of their bodies were covered properly. He told them how to dress so that they were prepared for the work they had to do, and so other people could identify or tell who the priests were.

They wore a breastplate, an ephod (a sleeveless garment), a robe, a skilfully woven tunic, a turban, and a sash. All the items that made up this physical dress for the priests represented holiness.

> "And you shall make holy garments for Aaron your brother, for glory and for beauty. ... And these are the garments which they shall make: a breastplate, an ephod, a robe, a skilfully woven tunic, a turban, and a sash. So they shall make holy garments for Aaron your brother and his sons, that he may minister to me as priest." (Exodus 28: 2, 4)

This teaches me that I too need to dress on the outside to cover my private parts and the rest of my body properly and in a way that prepares me for the work I have to do. I also see that what I wear can identify or show where I belong.

I need to dress in a certain way so that wherever I go, I show that I belong to God.

Priests are to be dressed on the outside (the body, externally), and also on the inside—spirit and soul (internally).

How can I dress the inside of me? I have to put on the spiritual clothing that God has for me. This whole outfit is called the *armour of God*. It is made out of a tough spiritual material that cleans, covers, and protects my spirit and soul against all of Satan's attacks. It gets me ready for the spiritual work I have to do.

Dylan's Uniform

Dylan's new alarm clock rang, telling him it was time to get up and get ready for school—much to his disappointment. He wanted to just roll over and hug his pillow a little longer, but again his alarm sounded. So Dylan got up, turned off the alarm, and headed to the bathroom and then to the breakfast table.

"Why do I have to put on a uniform for school? Why can't I just wear my jeans and T-shirt? It would be much more comfortable than those itchy shorts and shirt-jack that I have to wear. And then I could wear my favourite green T-shirt and jeans."

Mother hurriedly put breakfast before him. "Stop whining about your uniform. Hurry up, shower, and get dressed. We have to leave!"

Dylan quickly ate his breakfast, took a shower, and put on his uniform. He was not very happy to do it but nevertheless did it because he had to.

It was tour day, and the children were all going to the science fair and then to the park. Dylan was happy to be going out, until he got to their destination. There were lots of buses, and students from different schools. Dylan was not happy about the crowds, but he still looked forward to seeing everything.

The teachers urged the children to stay together. They were put in pairs and went off to explore the many tents displaying the creativity of scientific minds. They saw things that were made out of wood, such as furniture and toys that could move into unusual positions. They saw things that were made out of clay, such as pots, plates, and cups, which had electrical devices attached to them. They saw tablets, computers, and new game systems. Dylan was enjoying himself, but after a while the smells of the popcorn, hot dogs, and chicken mingling in the air made him feel quite hungry.

So it was not surprising that when Dylan saw the cotton candy being spun onto its stick, he did not notice his classmates moving on without him. Even the classmate he was paired with did not notice. When Dylan came to his senses, he realised he was surrounded by a lot of different uniforms but not a single one of his own. Dylan looked around frantically to spot one of his classmates or teachers but could not see through the thick blanket of students. Dylan did not know what to do, but he remembered the Lord and asked Him to help.

Suddenly he felt a hand take his, and when he looked up it was his teacher Mrs Roslyn. Dylan was happy to see her.

Mrs Roslyn was also happy to see Dylan. "Thank God I found you. I was looking around for a while, but then I saw your uniform and knew you were one of ours."

That's when Dylan understood why it was important to wear his uniform. His uniform showed where he belonged and what he was—a student of Chap Haven's Boys School.

9

The Armour of God, 1

The *armour of God* is the spiritual uniform for everyone who believes in God.

> Put on the whole armour of God, that you may be able to stand against the wiles of the devil. For we do not wrestle against flesh and blood, but against principalities, against powers, against the rulers of the darkness of this age, against spiritual hosts of wickedness in the heavenly places. Therefore take up the whole armour of God, that you may be able to withstand in the evil day, and having done all, to stand.
>
> Stand therefore, having girded your waist with truth, having put on the breastplate of righteousness, and having shod your feet with the preparation of the gospel of peace; above all, taking the shield of faith with which you will be able to quench all the fiery darts of the wicked one. And take the helmet of salvation, and the sword of the Spirit, which is the word of God. (Ephesians 6:11–17)

The first part of this armour that I must put on is the *helmet of salvation.*

 ## The Physical Helmet

A helmet protects my head from being injured. This is important because my head holds my brain, which controls my entire body. If the head and brain are badly injured, it is likely that my whole body will die.

 ## Kate's Helmet

Kate ran towards the rocky cliff. She could not wait to climb the rugged face to get to the top. Daddy had made sure he had all the tools he needed in his backpack. He needed a hammer and iron pitons to nail into the rock face as they climbed. He would then attach a line to it to hold them in case they slipped. Dad also would place a harness on Kate and make sure it was firmly attached to him for extra safety. Kate had never fallen while climbing, but Dad knew it was a good idea to have her attached to him just in case.

"Kate, where is your helmet?" Dad asked.

"I don't need it, Dad," Kate said. "I don't like the feel of it on my head, and I don't like having the straps under my chin."

"We've been through this before. You have to wear your helmet because it protects you—"

Kate broke in to complete the sentence she had heard many times. "It protects your head from getting hurt from the sharp points of the rock face."

Dad was not amused. "This is not a joke. A helmet protects your head and your brain. Your brain is in charge of your body. You need it working properly so that you can live. Besides, I even got you a nice girly one, pink with flowers and little hearts."

Kate did not protest anymore since she knew she could not win the argument. She set off to collect her helmet from the car.

Once they were both properly dressed for the adventure at hand, Dad and Kate were ready to start out.

"Follow me," Dad said. "Grip where I grip, and step where I step."

This was not news to Kate. She had been on many climbs with Dad and was sure she could climb to the top without Dad telling her every little thing she should do.

After climbing carefully for some time, when the pair had almost reached the top Kate decided that she had had enough of her helmet. After all, she was almost there. She thought it wouldn't matter if she took it off now. So while Dad was pounding in one of the iron pitons, Kate loosened the strap of her helmet with one hand. But when she tried to take it off, she couldn't get a good grip on it. In trying to stop the helmet from falling, Kate forgot all about her footing and slipped.

Dad felt the sudden tug, which also caused him to lose his footing and fall as well. Thankfully the pitons he nailed into the rock face were hammered in tight, and he was able to grip the rock face again.

Dad's heart was thumping loudly in his chest. He called out for Kate but got no response.

When Dad looked down, he saw Kate's limp body dangling at the end of the harness. Her helmet was off, and he knew she must be badly hurt. Dad immediately got his cell phone and called for help. Carefully and skilfully, Dad made his way down the rock face until he and Kate were on the ground again.

Dad flattened himself out on the ground and asked God to save his little girl's life. The ambulance arrived, and off they went to the hospital. It was two weeks before Kate woke up. She had injured her head so badly that the doctors were not sure she would be OK. When Dad saw Kate open her eyes, he was extremely happy and gave God thanks.

After Kate got out of the hospital she never forgot to put on her helmet when climbing. She now understood for the first time just how important it was to be dressed properly for a sport like rock climbing. Without a helmet, she could be seriously injured—or worse.

The Spiritual Helmet Is Salvation

The physical helmet for my head is made out of a hard plastic, but *salvation* is made out of Jesus.

It is made out of Jesus as *Saviour* and Lord.

Jesus is called *the Saviour* because He came to the earth to save me from the power of sin and free me from Satan. Jesus is called Lord because He is my King and ruler, and whatever He says to do I am to do it.

Every person is born with sin, so every single person needs *salvation*, "for all have sinned and fall short of the glory of God" (Romans 3:23). *Salvation* is a gift. It was paid for by Jesus with His life and is free to anyone who wants it. If you want it, all you have to do is ask Jesus, and it will be given to you. It is your choice, but you have to choose.

> Nor is there salvation in any other, for there is no other name under heaven given among men by which we must be saved. (Acts 4:12)

When I put on *salvation*, I put on Jesus. He is my covering and protection.

Joseph Gets Salvation

Joseph sat by himself on the bottom row of the pavilion. He hugged his legs as he thought about his life and what he had been doing. He felt sad inside because he had been lying to his dad every day. He told his dad that he would be late in getting home after school because he had extra lessons with his teacher. He wasn't doing well in his classes, and he knew that his dad really wanted him to do well and thought this lie would make his dad happy.

But the truth was, Joseph stayed behind after school to play cricket with his friends. Joseph had started this lie only two weeks ago, and at first he was happy. Now the fun of playing was gone. He felt sad for lying to his dad every day and was scared that his dad would find out what he was actually doing. Plus he really did not want to get punished. He hated being lashed and not being able to watch television.

Mr Allston, Joseph's teacher, saw him sitting in the pavilion. He noticed that Joseph looked really down.

"Hello, Joseph," Mr Allston said. "What's on your mind?"

Joseph was startled. He had not seen Mr Allston approach. "Hello, sir."

Mr Allston saw how nervous Joseph looked, so he asked the question again.

Joseph bowed his head. He did not know what to say. He did not want Mr Allston to think of him as a liar or to tell his dad the truth, but he was also tired of lying.

"You know, Joseph, you look like someone who has done

something he's not proud of. It's OK if you don't want to tell me, but I think you should talk to the Lord about it."

Joseph looked up at Mr Allston. He had not thought of talking to the Lord. After all, he thought the Lord must hate him for lying all the time.

"Are you saved, Joseph?" Mr Allston asked.

Joseph shrugged. "I don't know what you mean."

"Well, to be saved is to believe that God sent His Son Jesus into the world to die and to kill the power of sin, so that you could live and do what is right. It is to choose to live for God and not for Satan. When you ask for *salvation*, it means Jesus washes away all the bad things you have done before and gives you a new life in Him."

Joseph knew that he had done plenty of bad things and that he was nasty on the inside. "Why would Jesus love me? I'm a bad person. I tell lies, I call the other boys bad things, and I cheat when I'm doing a test."

Mr Allston could hear that Joseph was being honest. "Jesus loves you because you are part of His creation. God sent His Son Jesus into the world to save all those who would listen and believe in Him. He came to this dark, nasty world to free people from Satan and his lies. To do it, He had to give up His life and take the punishment for sin, which is death."

Mr Allston put his hand on Joseph's shoulder. "You see, Joseph, Jesus died on the cross so that you could truly live a life that is pleasing to God with His help. Jesus has the power and strength to do what is right all the time. The power of sin died that day on the cross, but Jesus still lives. When you put on Jesus, He will cover you, protect you, and help you."

Joseph could not believe it. This was the best news he had ever heard. "I thought He died to help the people back then when He was on the earth. I never thought Jesus died to help everyone who comes into the world, especially someone like me. What do I have to do to be saved?"

"You must believe in your heart that Jesus is God's Son."

"I believe that," Joseph said excitedly.

"You must believe that He died to take the power of sin away from you."

Joseph said, "I want Him to take away my sins. I do not want to do what is wrong anymore. I believe that Jesus has the power to do it."

"Good. Since you believe, all you have to do is ask Jesus for salvation, and He will give it to you."

Mr Allston got up and turned to leave, but before he did, he looked to Joseph again. "We've all done bad things, Joseph. I was a bully when I was in school. But Jesus called me, washed me, and covered me. He changed everything about me, and I'm glad He did."

As Mr Allston walked away, Joseph could not believe that his teacher had ever been a bad person. "Well," he said to himself, "if God can save Mr Allston, then He can save me too."

Joseph closed his eyes and spoke to the Lord from his heart. "I'm sorry, Lord, for all the bad things I did when I called others bad words and when I told lies to my dad. Please forgive me. I believe that You are Jesus, my Saviour and Lord, and I want to live for You and not for Satan. Thank you for loving me so much that You came to save me."

Joseph opened his eyes, took up his backpack, and headed home. On his way, he asked Jesus to give him the strength to tell the truth.

He walked straight up to his dad, determined not to tell any more lies.

Joseph waited for his dad to yell or to tell him his punishment, but instead his dad said, "Thank you for telling me the truth."

Tears rolled down Joseph's face. From that day on, Joseph was always glad for *salvation* and lived to please the Lord.

10

The Armour of God, 2

Another part of the armour of God that I put on is called the *belt of truth*.

> Stand therefore, having girded your waist with truth. (Ephesians 6:14)

The Physical Belt

A physical *belt* is made out of a strong material and goes around the centre of me, my waist. It holds my clothing in place and provides a place to attach useful things such as tools. It can also be used to discipline me.

In ancient Roman times, a soldier's belt held pieces of leather attached to the front for added protection of the lower parts of the body. The belt also had a scabbard attached to it, which held the soldier's sword or weapons.

 Kia's Belt

Kia pulled up her blue jeans. She zipped up and then buttoned the waistband, but they still sagged around her waist. Kia frowned because it was the third time she had tried on new pants that were a little too big in the waist. She did not know what to do.

Mother stood in the doorway, took one look at Kia, and said, "I know what will fix that problem."

Then she turned and walked down the corridor. Kia followed her mother into her room. Mother went to her drawer and pulled out a long leather strap.

"What's that?" Kia asked.

"It's a belt," Mother answered. "Hold still and I'll put it around the waist of your pants to keep them from falling."

The belt was made up of a long slender leather piece with a hard buckle in the front. When Mother was finished, Kia realised that her pants sat well on her waist now and felt comfortable.

Then her face changed to a frown again, which caught Mother's attention. "What's wrong now? Is it too tight?"

"No, it's not too tight. It's that I just remembered that Aunty Leah wanted me to bring my tools today so we could work in the workshop. Last time I watched her carve out a little bird on Mr Wilson's new dining room table that she made. Today she said she would teach me how to do it too."

Mother was puzzled. "Well, what's wrong with that? I thought you liked working in the workshop."

"I do, but I don't like having to carry my tools everywhere in my hands."

Mother smiled. Kia knew Mother must have an idea as to what to do. Mother always seemed to know just the right things to do to solve every problem.

Mother pulled a little box out of the closet. Inside was what looked like a little bag with pockets. It had all these sections where you could put a chisel, a little hammer, pencils, measuring tape, and anything else you needed.

Mother loosened Kia's belt and took it off. Then she attached the little bag to the belt and put it on again. Soon Kia had all her tools in the little tool bag on her waist. Now she was happy.

She gave her mother a big hug and exclaimed, "You're the best!"

Mother gave her a kiss on her forehead. "There, now you're ready. What did you learn in all this?"

Kia thought for a minute and then said, "I learnt that a belt is important because it can go all the way round me and can tighten up to keep my clothes up. Best of all, I can attach things to it to hold the tools I need."

Mother gave Kia a high five, and then they got in the car to go to Aunty Leah's house.

The Spiritual Belt Is Truth

What is truth? Truth is the plain, straight facts that say what really took place. It leaves nothing hidden or deliberately left out. It is opposite to a lie. Some examples of opposites are hot and cold, dry and wet, day and night, happy and sad, and good and bad.

For example, if you are told that Tom is wearing a blue shirt, and then when you see Tom, he is dressed in a blue shirt, is this truth or a lie? This is truth.

Sometimes you can tell part of a truth but hide the rest. Here's an example.

Jasper's food is gone, and his mother asks, "Did you eat all your food?"

Jasper says, "Well, it's all gone." He shows his mother the empty bowl. But under the table is Jasper's dog, Penny, and, yes, the bowl is empty, but it was Penny that ate all the food and not Jasper.

So was Jasper lying? Yes, Jasper was lying. He knew his mother was really asking him if *he* ate all his food, and he wanted her to believe that he did even though he knew he hadn't.

God wants me to speak the *truth*. This is part of His armour against Satan. When I tell a lie or leave out the truth, I open the door of my spiritual part for Satan to enter and stay there to cause harm.

Satan is a liar. He lies to me when he tells me that it is better to lie and save myself from being punished. He does this to make me afraid so that I think I am protecting myself or staying safe when in fact I am causing harm to myself. Sin is harmful to my spiritual part, just like a physical poison is harmful to all who swallows it.

Sin makes me feel afraid, ashamed, embarrassed, sick, and worried. And sin is also darkness. It makes me cloudy on the inside so that I cannot see or hear what the Lord says.

Truth does the opposite to what lying does. It gives me peace, strength, and health to my spirit, soul, and body, and it also helps me see, hear, and understand what is good and who God is.

Truth is the Word of God.

> The Word of God surrounds the whole of my spirit and soul.
> The Word of God holds the rest of the spiritual garment in place.
> The Word of God disciplines my spirit and soul.

The Word of God is where I get my tools and weapons to fight Satan.

All Scripture is given by inspiration of God, and is profitable for doctrine, for reproof, for correction, for instruction in righteousness, that the man of God may be complete, thoroughly equipped for every good work. (2 Timothy 3:16–17)

Then Jesus said to those Jews who believed Him, "If you abide in my word you are my disciples indeed. And you shall know the truth, and the truth shall make you free." (John 8:31–32)

Rick Lives the Truth

Rick opened his Bible to do his devotional reading time. The scripture Rick read was Ephesians 4:28: "Let him who stole steal no longer, but rather let him labour, working with his hands what is good, that he may have something to give him who has need."

Afterwards, Rick got ready and went off to school. At school, something caught his attention in mathematics class. It was an ornament dangling at the end of Matthew's keychain.

That would make a good addition to my collection, Rick thought.

The classroom was where Rick got most of his collection. He had taken pencils, erasers, sharpeners, and pretty much anything unusual. Unfortunately for Rick, most of the things he stole never lasted long at home. Rick always managed to break each thing, even though he tried not to.

Then it was time for Bible class. Mr Sane asked, "Who in this class has spent time with God today?"

Rick raised his hand proudly and said, "I have, sir. I did my devotional reading this morning."

Mr Sane smiled and asked Rick to share what he had read. Rick quoted the scripture from his Bible. He said, "Ephesians four, verse twenty-eight, says: 'Let him who stole steal no longer, but rather let him labour, working with his hands what is good, that he may have something to give him who has need.'"

Mr Sane leaned against his desk and asked Rick, "What does this truth mean to you?"

Rick was dumbfounded. He never actually thought about the meaning of the scriptures he had read.

Before Rick could answer, Mot raised his hand and said, "It means that if you are someone who steals things from people, you should stop doing it."

Then Jazz raised his hand and added, "It also means that instead of stealing, you should work so that you can have something to give to those in need."

Rick listened. He felt ashamed for what he had been doing. Before, he had thought of stealing as just a game, but now he saw it was a serious thing that was against God's Word.

Rick's heart changed that afternoon. He decided that he was no longer going to read the scriptures for the sake of saying he read them. He was going to do what the Word of God says to do.

After Rick got home, he asked his dad to help him find after-school work. Dad went with Rick around the neighbourhood, and by the end of the evening, Rick had lined up a set of jobs for each day of the week.

Soon Rick had saved enough money to pay back the classmates he had stolen from. He asked for their forgiveness and gave each of them a sum of money. The children willingly forgave Rick, and instead of stealing, Rick looked around school to see who needed pencils, erasers, lunch, a new school bag, or even a new pair of shoes.

Rick explained to Mr Sane what was in his heart to do. He wanted to help others but did not want them to know the money came from him. Mr Sane was happy to assist Rick in helping others. Rick gave the money to Mr Sane, who made sure the student in need was taken care of.

One day, Mr Sane asked Rick why doing this was so important to him.

Rick replied, "It's because God speaks the truth. His Word corrected me and taught me the right thing to do."

11

The Armour of God, 3

The next part of the armour God gives me to put on is the *breastplate of righteousness.*

> Stand therefore, having girded your waist with truth, having put on the breastplate of righteousness, and having shod your feet with the preparation of the gospel of peace; above all, taking the shield of faith. (Ephesians 6:14–16)

The Physical Breastplate

A physical breastplate guards the important parts of the body, such as the heart and lungs.

The heart is the part of me that pumps blood with oxygen to all the parts of my body so that they work correctly. The lungs take in air so that I can get oxygen into my body to give to my heart for use.

These two physical organs are very important because they work to keep my physical body alive. A person can live with a hurt leg, a hurt arm, or even with those parts missing, but a person cannot live without the heart or lungs.

The physical breastplate doesn't just cover the body like usual clothing that may be soft and comfortable but easily ripped or penetrated to reach the body. The physical breastplate is an extra covering that goes over everyday clothing and stays on. It is made of a very strong material to stop the enemy's weapons from breaking through to the skin and reaching the vulnerable parts.

Armour is used to protect a person in battle. Soldiers put on a *breastplate* when they fight against their enemy so that the important, softer, weaker parts of their bodies are not injured and they can continue fighting in the battle.

Fencing Foes

James was excited. It was his first fencing class. He was given the foil, helmet, and an outfit. First they did warm-up exercises, like stretching and running. Then it was time to hold the foils in hand.

A foil is like a long sword with a blade that is bendable at the end. For the sport of fencing, the foil has a flat rubber piece on the tip so that no one is cut with the sharp point.

James thought this was going to be an easy sport to learn—at least it looked that way when he watched it on television.

The instructor put them into pairs and instructed them how to move their wrist from side to side with the foil in hand. The instructor said, "This is called parrying. Parrying is used to push the other person's foil away so that your chest is not reached by the tip of their foil."

The instructor also told the children that when they got better at parrying, they would be able to stop any attack from their opponent.

One by one they had to stand before the instructor and try to parry away his attacks. The first time James got hit by the tip of the foil, it hurt. When James got home and took off his shirt, he saw that he was bruised on his chest by all the strikes that reached him in class.

James was surprised. He thought the clothing he wore was enough to protect him, but clearly it wasn't. When James showed his parents what had happened, they both said it would be necessary to get a breastplate of tougher material which would protect him from injury.

Dad was a tailor and knew he could make a nice breastplate out of leather which would protect James in the next class. James proudly wore the breastplate over his normal clothing. His classmates laughed even though each of them also got bruised in the first class.

James felt embarrassed and took off the breastplate. During the whole class, James endured being hit in the chest by the students and the instructor alike. After class, he put on the breastplate because he did not want his dad to know that he was embarrassed by what he had made for him.

On his way home, James spotted two of his fencing classmates duelling in an alley. This was strictly forbidden by their instructor. The boys were swinging wildly at each other.

James ran over to the boys. "Stop! You're not supposed to play with the foils. They're dangerous."

"No they're not," one of the boys replied.

Then the other boy pushed James out of the way and continued swiping. It was on one of these swipes that the foil hit the wall of the building they were next to, removing the hard protective rubber covering at the tip of the foil.

Not realising this, the boy lunged at the other. James jumped in the way, and the foil's sharp point hit his breastplate.

The boys froze in place with a gasp, until they relaxed and realised that if James was not wearing the breastplate, the foil would have pierced his chest and possibly caused grave injury to his organs. That also meant the other boy would have been seriously injured if James had not jumped in the way. From then on, James was proud to wear his breastplate, and none of his classmates gave him any trouble.

The Spiritual Breastplate Is Righteousness

What is *righteousness*? *Righteousness* is found with God and in no other place. It has to do with being right and good. To know what is right and good comes only by knowing God, because He alone is right, good and wise all the time.

To be right and good is to be correct and not wrong.

To be *wise* (as God is) is to know and understand everything. God is the only One who is wise. He knows and understands everything. God can see and hear everything, everywhere, all at once. This is because He made the world and everything in it, so He is the only one who knows everything about the world. He knows about all the plants, animals, and people.

People can discover or find plants and animals and say they've found a new plant or animal that no one knew about. But God knew about it from the beginning, because He was here from the beginning and made everything.

God knows how everything works. He made me, so He knows me better than I know myself. He knows how I think and feel. And there are some physical parts inside me that I do not know or understand, but God knows them all.

God is very wise, and there is no other person or thing that is like Him.

God calls the righteousness or wisdom of this world "foolishness" because we think we know what is right to think, say, and do, but without God our thinking, speaking, and doing is wrong and not right.

Righteousness is thinking the same way God thinks. It is saying the same things God says and doing the same things God does. Jesus, our Lord and Saviour, is the perfect example of thinking, speaking, and doing everything like God the Father.

If I want to know and do what is right, I need to listen and believe what God says. Believing God is also called righteousness.

> And behold, the word of the LORD came to him [Abraham], saying, "This one shall not be your heir, but one who will come from your own body shall be your heir." Then He brought him outside and said, "Look now toward heaven, and count the stars if you are able to number them." And He said to him, "So shall your descendants be." And he believed in the LORD, and He accounted it to him for righteousness." (Genesis 15:4–6)

Righteousness is a spiritual *breastplate* to my spirit and soul. It stays in place all the time so that I can know and see what is right and what is wrong, what is good and what is bad, and what is straight and what is crooked.

God's *righteousness* protects me from sin and saves me from Satan's traps. To keep this *breastplate of righteousness* in place, I must believe all that God says.

Amanda Believes God

Amanda walked through the park. It was her favourite place to be. As she walked, she thought about the situation she was in. She and her friend Melissa were like sisters. Their parents were close, so Amanda and Melissa kind of grew up together. Going to the same school and sharing the same class also made these two pretty much inseparable—until Natalie showed up.

Natalie was a transfer student to their class. She had beautiful dark skin and braided hair and was tall and strong. The first week of school, she was chosen to be on the basketball team, the volleyball team, and the swimming team. It wasn't long before everyone wanted to be Natalie's friend. But it was Melissa she got along best with and not Amanda.

Varying emotions flowed through Amanda in the days of Natalie's budding friendship with Melissa. She saw that Natalie was smart and strong, but she also saw that Natalie was rude and liked hurting other people's feelings. Amanda did not know how to warn Melissa about Natalie without coming across as just jealous.

Then Amanda remembered her Bible class teaching about taking everything to the Lord in prayer because He alone is *righteousness*, having all wisdom and power.

Amanda whispered to herself, "God will know what to do."

She found the nearest park bench, sat on it, and prayed. "God, thank you for being the One who has all wisdom and power. I do not know what to do. I do not know what to feel and think. I do not want to be jealous. I do not want to be angry. I want to think, feel, and do what's right. Please help me. I see that Natalie has a lot of talents, but she is very mean to others. I do not know how to tell Melissa about this. What do I do, Lord?"

Amanda felt the pain in her heart lift, and a peace came to her. She heard the Holy Spirit speak, and this was His question: "Do you love Melissa enough to tell her the truth no matter what?"

Then Amanda heard God's voice reminding her what 1 Corinthians 15:33 says: Do not be deceived: 'Evil company corrupts good habits.' Awake to righteousness, and do not sin; for some do not have the knowledge of God.

Amanda believed God and knew what God wanted her to do. She walked back to her dad, who was sitting quietly watching the ducks on the pond.

The next day, Amanda asked Melissa if she could speak to her alone. She talked to Melissa about what she saw in Natalie and about what 1 Corinthians 15:33 says.

Melissa listened quietly and then said, "What God says is true. I was really rude to Jenifer Curtis earlier, and my parents too. I never did that before."

Later that day, Melissa and Amanda spoke to Natalie and told her that she needed to stop being so rude to others. But Natalie shrugged and walked off.

Melissa turned to Amanda. "Thanks for being a good friend."

And Amanda turned to God with her heart and said, "Thank you for Your righteousness, Your right thinking, and Your right speaking, and thank you for helping me do what is right."

12

The Armour of God, 4

Now I will take up my *shield of faith.*

> Stand therefore, having girded your waist with truth, having put on the breastplate of righteousness … above all, taking the shield of faith with which you will be able to quench all the fiery darts of the wicked one. (Ephesians 6:14, 16)

 ## The Physical Shield

A physical *shield* is similar to a physical breastplate because it protects the body from getting injured by the weapons of the enemy. It differs in that it is not worn directly on the body. Unlike the physical breastplate, it is not fastened in one place. The physical shield is held in front of a person and is attached to the arm so the person can move it to protect any part at any time.

The physical shield is to be taken up and held. A person must choose to hold it.

Why must I take up my shield?
The physical shield guards.
It deflects attacks.
A physical shield makes it hard for a physical enemy to hit the body.
It pushes the enemy back.

Shields Up

Beatrice and her dad were looking in the children's section of the bookstore when customers coming brought the news.

They said, "There's an angry mob making its way through the streets! They will reach this street soon."

The store managers decided to lock the doors. They told the customers, and everyone agreed that it would be best until the police came to calm the situation. It seemed that other store owners on the street had made the same decision, as Beatrice could see them locking their doors.

One of the customers asked, "Why is there an angry mob?"

Another customer answered, "The owners of the apartment buildings in Nuret Village decided that they wanted to tear them down to build an amusement park. The tenants refused to leave, but a law was passed this morning that allowed the owners of the buildings to tear them down. All the tenants were given a short time to leave before the demolition began."

"No wonder they are so angry," responded the curious customer.

Then someone said, "Look outside—the policemen have arrived. It looks like they are going to take a stand here against the angry mob."

Beatrice saw the angry men and women making their way towards the policemen. She was glad to be indoors and held on tightly to her dad's leg.

Dad patted Beatrice's shoulder to comfort her.

Beatrice looked at the policemen. She could not see their faces because they were wearing helmets. They also had on special breastplates. But the thing that fascinated her most was the big metal shield attached to their arms.

"Daddy, why are the policemen dressed like that?" she asked.

"Because they don't want to get hurt, and—"

Before Dad could finish his sentence, he was interrupted by loud thumps that turned his attention again to the crowd.

Beatrice, her dad, and all the customers trapped in the book store watched as the mob threw rocks at the officers who were standing in their way. As the rocks came down, the officers raised their shields, and the rocks bounced off them.

Then one man went forward with a bat and swung at one of the officers, but the officer raised his shield and the bat broke into pieces when it hit the shield.

When the people saw that they could not hurt the officers with stones or their bats, they tried to push them down, but the shields were strong and the officers were able to push the crowd back. Finally, the chief of police took up a loudspeaker and told the people that they were going to start arresting them for trying to hurt the policemen.

Soon the crowds were all gone, and the streets were clear and safe enough for Beatrice, her dad, and all the other customers to make their way home. As they went, Beatrice thought about the shield and how much she wanted one.

The Spiritual Shield Is Faith

What is faith? *Faith* is unshakeable belief in something or someone. God alone can be trusted with everything because He already knows everything. He can hear everything and has the answers for everything. Our trust is to be in God alone and not in our own strength, because we have no strength apart from God.

Faith is a spiritual shield that has to be picked up with my spiritual part. It must be held in place over what I think, what I want to have or do, what I learn, and what I feel. It guards my spirit and soul from attacks from the enemy; it pushes the enemy back and repels or deflects his attacks. Without having *faith*, I cannot please God.

> Without faith it is impossible to please Him, for he
> who comes to God must believe that He is, and that
> He is a rewarder of those who diligently seek Him.
> (Hebrews 11:6)

The way of getting faith is to hear the Word of God. Believe it and know that it is true, ask God for help to do it by praying, and live it by obeying.

Faith is believing and trusting God and His Word even if I don't know how something will work out. *Faith* changes the way I think, feel, speak, and live. It takes away doubts and fears and gives me peace and strength because I know God loves me and will always help me. "For *we*"—those who believe in God—"walk by faith, not by sight" (2 Corinthians 5:7, emphasis added).

Here's a poem that helps me remember what faith is.

Faith
Faith is the truth that I hear.
It is God's Word that draws near.
When I take it in,
It turns my heart from sin,
Changing my thoughts, words, and actions too,
So that in God little and great things I will do.

No Matter What

Principal Atlas stood with the microphone in hand and uttered the message for which he had the whole school body assembled to hear.

He said, "Bullying will not be tolerated in this school. If you are being bullied, you need to let your teachers know."

Some students shifted uncomfortably.

Principal Atlas continued, "Please remember that you need to have at least one witness with you so that we are able to fairly judge the situation."

After more general announcements, the students were dismissed and made their way back to their classes.

Johanna thought about what Principal Atlas had said. She was one of those students who were being bullied. She was being bullied by a boy named Marty. However, she did not have any witnesses.

Johanna explained this to her teachers. They kept an eye on Marty but never caught him at a time when he was doing anything to Johanna.

Maybe it was because Marty was very clever. He always made it appear that whatever he did was accidental, not deliberate, like when he bumped into Johanna now and again. There were also times he caused her to trip, but no one saw or could identify who had actually done it, since there was too much of a crowd around.

But Johanna knew it was Marty because he would find little moments to whisper things like "Watch your step" or "Why do you always trip up so easily?"

Why did this begin? It was because Johanna walked into the classroom unexpectedly and caught Marty stealing another student's wallet from his backpack. He knew that Johanna saw, so he put the wallet back, but since that day Johanna had been his target.

Johanna was very upset. One Saturday, after watching her mope around the house the entire morning, Granny finally said, "That's enough, Johanna. Let's talk."

Johanna curled up on the couch and placed her head on Granny's shoulder.

"Tell me what is going on, sweetie," Granny said.

"It's Marty," replied Johanna.

"Your mum and dad have spoken to the teachers, and they are keeping an eye on him, aren't they?" Granny asked.

"Yes, but he doesn't do anything when the teachers are around, and I have no witnesses at times he does do something."

"Johanna, have you forgotten who God is? Isn't He the one who sees and knows all things? Isn't He the one you can trust no matter what? You need to have faith in God."

Granny believed in God. She had great faith in God and knew that He would always provide all the answers to every situation.

Granny continued, "Faith is our shield against doubts, worries and fears. We are protected and strengthened when we believe that our God is with us and that He keeps His word."

Granny always encouraged Johanna to trust everything God said and to pray. And that is what Johanna did. She wanted to live by faith no matter what she saw or felt. She wanted to trust God like Granny did.

Johanna prayed, "God, I am glad that You see and hear everything. I have You as my witness. Help me. Let everyone see the truth about Marty."

After praying, Johanna wasn't so upset anymore. She felt the worry and anger being pushed away, and what replaced it was peace and happiness.

However, time went by, and nothing changed.

One day she asked Granny, "Why does it seem sometimes that when you pray, nothing happens?"

Granny replied, "If you are asking God something that agrees with His Word which you believe, then you simply have to trust Him while you are waiting for your answer."

"Yes Granny," replied Johanna.

She had two parts right. She was asking something that agreed with what God said, and she believed what God's Word said. But she was not very good at waiting. It seemed like it was taking too long, day by day, and week by week, for an answer to this problem to come. Johanna realised that waiting on God was the part of having faith that she had to learn.

A few days afterwards, a new boy came to the school. His nickname was Muscle. Everyone understood why as they looked at his tall and muscular stature.

One morning as Johanna was walking along the corridor, she heard a thump and a groan. When she looked by the stairway, she saw that Muscle was punching Marty over and over again.

"Stop it!" Johanna yelled. Then she yanked Muscle's shirt so that he fell backwards. Muscle got up quickly, looked around to see if anyone had seen, and then he ran off, leaving Johanna and Marty.

Marty glared at Johanna angrily, got up, and left.

Later that day Marty was still angry. Maybe it was at the thought of owing Johanna some sort of thanks. Whatever the reason, he could not contain himself. When Marty saw her in the classroom, he blurted out, "Johanna, don't think that this changes anything. I will still trip you up and knock you into the wall whenever I please."

Everyone heard him, including the teacher who was standing behind him. There were so many witnesses now that there was no doubt in Johanna's mind that Marty would receive the rightful punishment he deserved.

Johanna could not wait to tell Granny the news.

"Granny, God who sees all things made a way for everyone to see the truth about Marty. It wasn't easy going through it, or waiting for God's answer, but I was glad that I did."

Granny asked Johanna what she learnt about having faith.

Johanna replied, "I learnt that having faith is to trust what God says even if things don't seem to change right away, and, I learnt that this is what it means to walk by faith and not by sight."

13

The Armour of God, 5

The next part of the armour God gives me to put on is the *sword of the Spirit.*

> And take the helmet of salvation, and the sword of the Spirit, which is the word of God. (Ephesians 6:17)

The Physical Sword

A physical sword is used to defend or attack. It is used to cut an enemy in battle in order to wound or kill that enemy. A physical sword is made up of a handle and a blade. The handle is there so that you can get a good grip to control the sword correctly.

The blade must be sharp. If it is dull, it will not cut through an enemy in a way that quickly stops that enemy.

You must also know how to use the sword before you take it up.

A sharpened sword is extremely dangerous, and if you take it up without knowing how to use it properly, you can be injured. Only those who are trained or prepared can use a sword skilfully with knowledge and understanding of how to hold it and when and where to strike.

The Sharp Sword

Gavin practised with his sword to get ready for the martial arts showcase. Each member of his club had to choose a weapon to become skilful with. Gavin chose the sword because he liked the beauty of its handle and the design of its blade. Before Gavin could get a sword with a real blade, he had to practise many months with a wooden one and show his instructor that he had the understanding and control of how to use it.

Jonathan enjoyed watching his older brother practise in the empty garage. He would watch until it was time to go to bed.

Gavin warned Jonathan, "Never pick this sword up. It is not a toy." And after he thought Jonathan was out of sight, he would hide it on a high shelf in the garage.

But of course, Jonathan was very curious about where his big brother hid the sword. So one day he said, "Gavin, I have homework to do. I am going to my room."

Gavin watched as Jonathan left the garage.

Jonathan entered the house through the front door but exited through the back door. Then he made his way carefully back to the outside of the garage. Jonathan peeped through one of the windows and smiled. He had gotten his prize—the sword's hiding place was now known.

One afternoon, when Jonathan was sitting on the floor to work on a school project called "flying in the sky," he decided to make a glider with a harness for one of his toy soldiers to hold on to. Jonathan reached the point of having a stable frame, but now he needed to attach fabric to it. Jonathan tried and tried but could not tear the fabric with his hands. Then he got a pair of scissors, but they were too dull and would not cut the fabric either.

So guess what came into Jonathan's mind—Gavin's new sword!

"That should do it," he said to himself. And with that he ran to the garage, got the ladder, and climbed up until he reached the place where Gavin had stashed the sword for safekeeping.

Jonathan ran back into the house with the case and quickly opened it. He smiled as he looked at the beautiful carvings in the handle of the sword lying in its case.

Then he picked it up and felt its weight. "This is heavier than it looks," he muttered. It never looked this heavy when his brother was swinging it around!

Jonathan looked down at his arms. "I definitely need more muscles," he whispered and then chuckled.

Jonathan tried to get the sword to cut the thick fabric, but it was too heavy for him to hold with one hand while trying to hold the fabric with the other hand. Then Jonathan had an idea. He got two dining room chairs and separated them so that there would be a space between for the fabric to stretch across. Then he put books on top of the fabric on each chair so that it stayed nice and straight for him to cut.

Jonathan had seen his brother swipe downwards many times and thought that he would be able to do it too. So he held the sword high above his head with both hands and then swiped downwards. The sword did indeed cut through the fabric—but it didn't stop there.

"Mummy! Mummy!" Jonathan screamed repeatedly. "Help me!"

Mummy entered the room and immediately sped into action. She grabbed the nearby kitchen towels and ran to get larger ones. She carefully and tightly wrapped them around Jonathan's leg. Then she grabbed her cell phone and car keys, lifted Jonathan into the car, and raced to the emergency section of the hospital. Gavin and their dad were already waiting for them there because Mummy had called them on the way.

The doctor was called immediately, and Jonathan was rushed into surgery. A few hours later, they were told the good news by the surgeon.

"Jonathan will be OK. His wound will heal, and he will be able to use his leg again. However, he will need to have a few therapy sessions to strengthen it again after it heals."

Jonathan learnt a lesson that he would never forget. He learnt that a sword is a serious weapon and that it should only be used by someone who is skilled with it.

The Spiritual Sword Is the Word of God

The *spiritual sword* that I need inside me is the Word of God, and the One who knows how to use it skilfully is God, the Holy Spirit.

This is why I need the Holy Spirit living inside me. He helps me understand what the scriptures mean, and when I understand and believe the scriptures, He takes up the Word of God with all His power and strength and cuts Satan's lies into pieces.

When I understand and believe the Word of God, the Holy

Spirit raises it to block out Satan's lies from entering me, lies that would steal from, kill, and destroy me, or lies that would use me to steal from, kill, and destroy others.

> For the word of God is living and powerful, and sharper than any two-edged [physical] sword, piercing even to the division of soul and spirit, and of joints and marrow, and is a discerner of the thoughts and intents of the heart. And there is no creature hidden from His sight, but all things are naked and open to the eyes of Him to whom we must give account. (Hebrews 4:12–13)

> This is the word of the Lord to Zerubbabel: "Not by might nor by power, but by my Spirit," says the Lord of hosts. (Zechariah 4:6)

The Word of God Cuts

Jane rolled in bed from side to side. She was in such turmoil. Jane had been sick for the whole week. She went from having a cough to having a fever and a worse cough. Then her chest and stomach started hurting too, followed by vomiting. Oh yes, the vomiting! Things got worse for Jane from that time on.

Mother tried to comfort Jane by reading her favourite book to her and by making her some warm soup, but nothing was able to take away the pain she had in her whole body.

Then Liam walked in. "Hi, Mum. Hi, Jane. We just got back from church."

Jane waved hello to Liam, who made his way onto her bed and next to her.

"What are you doing?" Mother asked. "Get down from there and let your sister rest."

But Liam just kept on chatting to his sister. "Guess what I learnt at church today, Janey? I learnt that if I believe what God says in His

Word, the Holy Spirit will take it up and cut Satan's lies to pieces. Isn't that cool?"

Liam got right up to Jane's head and said, "I'm going to pray for you, and you're going to be healed because the Holy Spirit will use God's words to destroy the sickness in your body."

Jane said, "You already prayed for me three times this week, Liam, and nothing happened."

"I know, Jane, but I didn't use the Word of God those three times. Well, only once, but even then I didn't really think about it as I was saying it. I didn't really believe it, but now I do. Please let me pray again."

Jane could not resist the eager little blue eyes staring into her face. "OK, Liam, go ahead."

Liam clapped his hands with joy. "Remember, Jane, you are to believe what God says too, OK?"

"I will."

Then Liam prayed, "God, thank you for my sister, Jane. Thank you for giving us your Word as a sword to cut Satan's lies to pieces. God, Your Word says that greater is He who is in us than he who is in the world. I thank You that Your Word also says that healing belongs to your children. Jane is one of your children, God. She believes in You. So, sickness, go away and leave her body. I ask this in the name of Jesus. Amen."

Jane's chest and stomach immediately stopped hurting, and the fever was gone.

Jane sat up, weak and tired but happy. She cried out, "I'm healed, Liam! I'm healed!"

Mother ran into the room to see the two siblings clapping with jubilation. Normally this would not have been a big deal, but today it was— just a few moments ago, Mother had left a crumpled-up Jane lying in bed.

"What just happened?" Mother asked.

Liam ran up to his mother and, doing chopping motions with his hands, blurted out, "Jane's healed 'cause the Holy Spirit took up the Word of God and whacked Satan's lies to pieces!"

✎ What Does It Mean to Be Holy?

The Holy Spirit is called "holy" because that is what He is. To be holy means to be pure and clean.

"Pure" means not mixed with something else; for example, there is pure orange juice, which means you squeezed oranges and did not add anything to it. You did not add water, sugar, or any other fruit to it.

You can also have pure leather clothing or accessories, such as handbags. This means those things are only made of leather from animal skins and not from any other material, such as cotton from a plant or silk from the cocoon of a type of caterpillar, and no other material was added or used.

I need to have a pure spirit for God, the Holy Spirit, to live and work in me freely and easily. I can have this by remembering who the Holy Spirit is and giving Him what He likes and not what He hates.

When I am at school, I try not to cheat in class, boast, tell lies, or be rude to my teachers. And when I am home, I choose what I watch and listen to, what I play, what I do on the internet, what I text, and what I read, knowing that I belong to God and that His home in me is to be a clean one.

> Finally, brethren, whatever things are true, whatever things are noble, whatever things are just, whatever things are pure, whatever things are lovely, whatever things are of good report, if there is any virtue and if there is anything praiseworthy—meditate on these things. (Philippians 4:8)

Or you can think of it this way. You would not like anyone to bring smelly, rotting garbage and dump it in the place you live. It would stink up the whole place and encourage nasty rodents, and you would not want to stay and work in that place. Sin is like that smelly, rotting garbage with rodents and all assorted creeping things. It stinks up the whole of your spirit and soul and limits what the Holy Spirit can do there.

The Holy Spirit likes a clean, fresh-smelling environment of truth, faith, true repentance, and righteousness, and so you need to practise such things to keep His home clean.

> Or do you not know that your body is the temple of the Holy Spirit who is in you, whom you have from God, and you are not your own? For you were bought at a price; therefore glorify God in your body and in your spirit, which are God's. (1 Corinthians 6:19–20).

🐾 A Clean Heart

The seatbelt sign came on, and Joe and his younger brother, Reece, buckled their seatbelts because the cabin attendants were checking to make sure that everyone was buckled in. Soon they were in the air, on their way to New York to spend the Christmas holidays with their big sister, Patricia. She had left Barbados to study in New York and ended up liking it so much that she decided to live there.

As the airplane made its way through the sky, the cabin attendants went around asking if anyone wanted anything to eat or drink. They said that each person would be given only one plate of food and one snack and that if you wanted anything else, you would have to pay for it.

Joe and Reece ate their food and snack and then they played their game apps on their iPads.

A little later, another cabin attendant came by with a tray of snacks. "Did you two have your snack with your meal already?"

Joe said yes, but Reece said no.

Reece pointed to what he wanted, and the cabin attendant gave it to him. Then she quickly moved on to the other rows of passengers.

"Why did you tell her that?" Joe asked.

Reece took a bite of the cake and smiled. "I like cake."

"That's not the point, Reece. You lied to her, and it's not funny or right."

Reece shrugged and finished his cake.

Later, the cabin attendants came round with earphones so that anyone who wanted to watch a movie could buy them. One took the money, and the other handed them out. Joe paid, but Reece didn't. He said he did not want to watch the movie. But when the cabin attendant came round to hand Joe the headphones, Reece stuck out his hand and took a pair too.

The angry look on Joe's face wiped the grin right off Reece's.

"It's only earphones, no big deal," Reece stated.

Joe tried to keep his voice down while still yelling at his younger brother. "No big deal! Stealing is no big deal? Didn't you listen to anything in the lesson we had on staying pure by the choices we make?"

Reece shrugged. "Get real, Joe, nobody really does that!"

Reece stuck the earphones in his ears, but Joe angrily yanked them out.

"I'm your big brother, and I tell you the truth. I have asked the Lord to take away my sins and make me clean because I want to live for Him. I want Him to rule over me. And I've learnt that it makes me stronger inside when I read the Word and live by it. It's not a fairy tale. It's true. I use to lie and cheat, but now I really like telling the truth and doing my own work."

Reece turned away and looked out the window, but Joe continued talking. "If you want to fight Satan and win, you need the Holy Spirit living in you. He only lives and works in a place that is clean and pure. You get clean by first repenting and then living by the Word of God. And you stay pure by the choices you make to please God every day." Then he asked, "Do you think Mum or Dad would be happy with you?"

"They're not here," Reece muttered.

"No. But God is always here and anywhere you go. He sees and hears you all the time. When you have a choice to do good or bad and you choose to do good because you know it pleases God, the Holy Spirit is happy with you and can teach and give you strength to fight Satan."

Reece leaned against the window. He wished he could ignore his brother, but he couldn't. He did remember hearing that he had to repent and live a pure life so that the Holy Spirit could live in him to fight Satan. He just never thought it was something that children were actually to do.

Reece looked at Joe, who was only two years older, and he remembered how his brother behaved previously and how much he had changed since he believed in God.

The two brothers did not say anything to each other for the rest of the trip. When the plane landed, the cabin attendant came to get them to take them where they needed to go, since they were not travelling with an adult.

"Excuse me," Reece said. "I need to pay you for my extra snack and earphones."

She was surprised, and so was Joe.

Joe whispered to Reece, "What made you do that?"

Reece turned to his brother. "I want the Holy Spirit to be working in me all the time, and that means I have to be clean and pure, right?"

"Right," Joe said with a smile.

14

The Armour of God, 6

Now I want to know what it means to have *feet prepared with the gospel of peace.*

> Stand therefore, having girded your waist with truth, having put on the breastplate of righteousness, and having shod your feet with the preparation of the gospel of peace; above all, taking the shield of faith with which you will be able to quench all the fiery darts of the wicked one. (Ephesians 6:14–16)

The Physical Feet

My physical *feet* are important because they keep me steady, stop me from falling, and carry me everywhere.

I have to prepare my feet for everywhere I take them. *Prepare* means to get ready. My physical feet are *prepared* or made ready for where they are to go or what they are to do.

I *prepare* my feet for school, football, diving, or ballet by washing them and dressing them in the correct footwear.

Getting my feet ready in the correct way is very important so that I do not suffer injuries.

 ## The Run

Danielle looked through the glass doors of the tall cabinet standing in the school hall. She looked at all the trophies and medals from the many years the students of Bridge High School had been competing with other schools in various sports, such as gymnastics, cricket, football, track and field, and swimming. Some of the trophies and medals were also for academic competitions in spelling, art, composition, and social studies.

Danielle wanted to have her name on a trophy in this huge cabinet someday. Coming up was the track and field interschool competition. Danielle practised by running long distances in the mornings before school and in the evening with her dad. He taught her how to breathe deeply and how to pace herself when she ran. If she ran too fast too soon, she would get too tired and not be able to finish the race, and if she ran too slowly, she would be left behind and not be able to catch up in time to have a chance at winning.

The day before the competition, her dad decided to take her out on a run through the park, along the beach, and through the next neighbourhood before returning home. Danielle enjoyed this very much, but just as she was approaching the next neighbourhood, she felt her shoe shift in a strange way. She slowed down and then stopped, as Dad had also taught her that it was not good to stop suddenly when running. He said the leg muscles needed to cool down so that they would not get injured.

Dad walked up to Danielle and spoke through his deep breathing. "What's wrong?"

"The bottom of my shoe has broken open," Danielle replied.

"Oh dear," Dad said. "All the shoe stores in this area are closed. You can't run in those anymore."

"It's all right." Danielle sighed. "I'll just wear my other soft shoes instead."

"No, you can't, Danielle. Those are not fit for running. You'll have to see if any of your cousins have running shoes that you can borrow."

Danielle did not like that idea. She did not like asking anyone to borrow anything, especially something like shoes. Her shoes were always very smelly after a long run, and she did not want to wear anyone else's smelly shoes.

The two stretched and walked home. The next morning, Danielle was glad that Dad was still asleep when she left with Mum for school.

The children from all the different schools were taken by bus to the stadium where they would run against each other. Danielle looked forward to competing. She had practised and was sure that she would win a medal that day.

When it was time to get ready for the races, Danielle changed into her sports uniform and put on her soft shoes. The coach was so busy organising everyone that he did not notice that Danielle was not wearing the correct footwear.

The athletes' hearts pounded as they awaited the whistle that would signal the start of the race.

Then suddenly the whistle blew and the children ran. They would have to run five laps, so it was important to breathe well and keep a good pace. Danielle kept up well enough and soon overtook each one in the pack. Then the final lap came and it was time to sprint to the end as fast as they could. Danielle pushed and pushed, but the pain in her feet stopped her from going as fast as she could. Soon she was overtaken by two people.

Danielle was very disappointed. She did not want third place. She knew she could have won, but more painful than losing first place were the sharp pains shooting through her feet. She sat on the grass and gently pulled off her soft shoes. Her feet were red and swollen. Danielle began to cry. She did not even imagine trying to walk on them now. Soon the coach and her teacher were by her side. They lifted her to a cooler spot and called her dad.

When the coach examined her feet, he said, "What shoes were you wearing?"

Danielle, embarrassed, pointed to the shoes.

The coach's eyes bulged with horror. "What! Danielle, where are your running shoes? You know you can't use just anything to run in."

Tears flowed down Danielle's face. She knew it was her fault she was in so much pain. She should have asked her cousins for help, as her Dad said.

Danielle's dad was soon by her side. She could see that he was concerned but also angry with her for being disobedient. "I think that you've learnt your lesson the hard way."

From then on Danielle always made sure her feet were prepared correctly for what she had to do.

The Spiritual Feet

My physical feet need to be prepared correctly for what they are going to do. This is also the same for my *spiritual feet* that have to be prepared for every situation I face and everything I have to do. My spiritual feet are my spirit and soul, which make up the spiritual part of me. I have to prepare my spiritual part with the gospel and live by this truth every day.

All scripture is valuable and important. The *gospel* within the scripture is the message of salvation. It tells me how Jesus came to the earth, lived, and died on the cross to set me free from the power of sin, and it tells me of how He was then raised to life and went to be with God in heaven. The gospel also tells me that Jesus will come again.

> "Let not your heart be troubled; you believe in God, believe also in me. In my Father's house are many mansions; if it were not so, I would have told you. I go to prepare a place for you. And if I go and prepare a place for you, I will come again and receive you to myself; that where I am, there you may be also. And where I go you know, and the way you know."
>
> Thomas said to Him, "Lord, we do not know where You are going, and how can we know the way?" Jesus said to him, "I am the way, the truth, and the life." (John 14:1–6)

This gospel can also be called the *salvation message* or the *good news* from God.

News is good when it means something nice or helpful for me. For example, if you could not walk because your legs did not work, it would be good news to know there was a doctor who was able to make you walk. Or if you could not see, it would be good news to hear that there was someone who could give you sight.

The gospel is good news to all of us—every boy, girl, man, and woman. It is good news to us because we hear that we are all born with the same death sentence or punishment for sin, which is eternal death. Then we hear that there is a cure—Jesus, who washes and takes away all our sins and makes our spirits and souls clean. He doesn't make them clean and leave them empty. He puts His thoughts and ways into our spirit and soul.

> Therefore, if anyone is in Christ, he is a new creation; old things have passed away; behold, all things have become new. (2 Corinthians 5:17).

This *gospel* or good news tells me that Jesus takes away my eternal death and gives me eternal life, which begins inside me while I am here on earth.

> The next day John saw Jesus coming toward him, and said, "Behold! The Lamb of God who takes away the sin of the world!" (John 1:29)

> And this is eternal life, that they may know You, the only true God, and Jesus Christ whom You have sent. (John 17:3)

Gaston Learns to Trust God

Gaston woke early with thoughts of all that he wanted to do that day. It was the first day Dad had off work in a long time, and Gaston was excited because Dad had said, "We can do whatever you want for the whole day."

Gaston heard a voice within him say, "Gaston, you need to pray now before you get ready to leave."

But Gaston was irritated to hear such a thing. He had no time to stop. Gaston answered within himself, "I will pray later."

He ran down the stairs and opened the door to the storage cupboard in the corridor. He rummaged through the shelves for the fishing rods, the broad hats, the buckets, and all the other things he would need to make a perfect fishing day.

Gaston turned round and noticed Dad standing in the doorway, smiling. "I see you already know what you want to do today," Dad said.

Gaston grinned. Dad reached to the higher shelves for the boxes of tools they would need.

Soon the truck was loaded and the two were off, singing their favourite songs as they went. But even as they sang, Gaston heard a voice within him say, "Have Dad check the boat's engine."

Gaston dismissed the thought by replying within himself, "Dad recently had the boat repaired, so it's all right now."

The two packed the supplies onto the boat, and Dad started up the engine. The boat rocked from side to side as they made their way into the deep. It was a beautiful day indeed. The sun shone brightly, and the colour of the sea reminded Gaston of a beautiful painting he saw in his aunt's art gallery.

"Can we go for a swim after we catch some fish?" Gaston asked.

Dad laughed and said, "Of course, son."

The pair sat with their fishing rods dangling in the sea. They chatted about school and Gaston's favourite books. Gaston told his dad about the dream he had of becoming a pilot for the hurricane hunters.

"That sounds dangerous," Dad said. "We'll have to pray about that and ask God if that's what He wants you to do."

Gaston looked at his dad.

"Son, to have salvation is to have a real relationship with God where He is the One who teaches and guides you every day. After all, He is the way, the truth, and the life."

"What does having a real relationship with God mean?" Gaston asked.

"It means that you allow God, the Holy Spirit, to prepare and rule over your spiritual feet."

Gaston giggled and exclaimed, "My spiritual feet!"

Dad smiled and said, "Yes, your spiritual feet are your spirit and soul. It is here that God communicates with you. He makes you able to hear and see Him. The more you listen and do all He says to you, personally, and from the Bible, the more He can use you to spread His truth through what you say and do."

Just as Dad was speaking, a loud noise came from the boat's control console. When they reached the area, they saw smoke and smelt what appeared to be wires burning.

"Oh no!" Dad yelled. "Bring the fire extinguisher."

As Dad put out the fire, Gaston suddenly remembered the voice within that he had ignored from the start of that day. Gaston knew it was the Holy Spirit who had urged him to pray and to ask Dad to check the boat. If he had paid attention to the Holy Spirit by listening and being obedient with his spirit, soul, and body, this would not have happened.

Gaston felt terrible inside. He said, "Dad, I have a confession to make. God told me to pray and that something was wrong with the boat, but I didn't listen."

"Don't worry," Dad said. "This will help you to listen the next time the Holy Spirit speaks to you. He's preparing your spirit and soul for what God has for you to do. You will learn to trust Him, son. I have had to learn to do this too."

Dad reached into his bag and pulled out his walkie-talkie. He looked at Gaston and said, "The Holy Spirit told me to pack this and to have my brother keep his with him today."

They both laughed and hugged.

Gaston was thankful that his Dad had been prepared as a result of believing God's Word and obeying what the Holy Spirit said.

What Is Peace?

Peace is freedom and relationship with God.

Peace is freedom from the guilt and condemnation of sin that weighs me down inside my spirit and soul. I can only have this peace when Jesus becomes my Saviour and Lord. This peace is kept with God when I agree with all that He says in His Word. My agreement with God is seen in the way I think, speak, and do things. By agreeing with God, I am able to have a deep relationship with Him.

Everyone is born blind, lame, deaf, and dead on the inside because of the sin in them, and anyone who does not get salvation and does not believe in God stays blind, lame, deaf, and dead inside their spirit and soul. They will be like the Pharisees, who had physical eyes that worked but were called "blind Pharisees" because they could not spiritually see, hear, or live the truth of God. Such a person is weighed down and covered in guilt and condemnation.

But if anyone chooses to go to Jesus to be saved, He will make that person able to see, hear, and *walk* in—that is, live—the truth. This *gospel* is *peace*; it is real and not false.

False peace comes from Satan, who tries to make me believe that even though I have done something wrong, it's really not that big a deal, or it's OK because everybody does the same thing.

Peace I leave with you, my peace I give to you; not as the world gives do I give to you. Let not your heart be troubled, neither let it be afraid. (John 14:27)

Perfect Peace

Cassie's spirit, soul, and body ached. She felt the heaviness of what she'd done. She wished she could take that whole time back and make it like it never happened, but she couldn't.

The worst thing for Cassie was that God had seen her disobedience, and this made her sad. Cassie knew the only thing to do would be to come clean. She remembered God's Word in 1 John 1:9: "If we confess our sins, He is faithful and just to forgive us *our* sins and to cleanse us from all unrighteousness."

Cassie apologised to God and made up her mind that she would speak with the principal about what she had done.

Cassie had broken the school rules. She had gone into the computer room with her friends without permission. It seemed like fun at first, and everyone was laughing and having a great time, but Cassie knew it was wrong. She found it hard to have a good time. In fact, she was happy when it was time to leave.

Then Jade tapped Cassie on the shoulder as they were leaving the computer room and said, "Come on, Cassie, you have to learn to live a little. You can't be so boring. Only boring people follow the rules all the time. Besides, all the second and third years are doing it."

Now it was the next morning, and Principal Parris stood on the platform for school assembly. Cassie's plan was to approach him after assembly was over. She knew what the punishment was for not following the school rules: the offender was not allowed to play at lunch breaks but instead had to help the janitor clean the bathrooms and help the gardener clean up any litter around the school grounds. Still, Cassie was determined to follow the Word of God.

Principal Parris waited for all the students to give him their full attention, and then he said, "It has been brought to my attention that there are some of you who have been entering the computer room to play video games. I'm not going to ask those who have done so to stand on the platform, but I will give all of you the opportunity to stop doing it. I forgive all those who have done this already. So from now on, you all have a clean slate. But if any of you go in from this day on, you will be punished."

Cassie was relieved. This was good news. She felt the weight of her guilt evaporate into nothingness. She was free from feeling so scared of what people would think of her, and she was free from being upset with herself for doing the wrong thing. There was now peace in Cassie's spiritual part, and she was able to breathe easy again. She had apologised to God, and God had made a way for her to be freed by the principal.

The next day, Cassie's friend Jade said, "Let's go in. He doesn't really know who's going into the computer room. He's just trying to scare us."

"Maybe," Cassie said, "but I know that Jesus died for me so that I could do what is right. The feeling I have when I do anything that doesn't agree with Him is enough punishment for me."

Cassie's friends went on without her, and sure enough, they were caught—and you know what they had to do as their punishment.

Cassie learnt that having peace meant listening to and doing what God says.

15

Put on the Whole Armour of God

When I put on the whole armour of God, I am putting on:

* salvation
* truth
* faith
* righteousness
* the Word of God
* the gospel of peace

Just as I make sure I am completely dressed before going to school or out with friends, I must make sure that I am completely dressed spiritually. If I am missing or lacking part of this *spiritual armour*, I will have weak areas where Satan can attack me.

> Therefore take up the whole armour of God, that you may be able to withstand in the evil day, and having done all, to stand. (Ephesians 6:13)

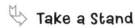 Take a Stand

Simon put his cricket gear together and then sat to pray. He said, "God, please help me to do well today, not only in my batting, bowling, and running but in my attitude towards the other players—my teammates and those of the other team.

"Help me to remember Your Word so that it is in my heart and also in my mouth. Help me today to share the gospel with others and not to be afraid. Let my faith be in You always that I should do what is right and live by Your truth."

When Simon was finished praying, he heard his neighbour George calling out to him. It was time to go. Simon picked up his bag and off he went.

The match went well for Simon and George's team, and they won. As was the custom, the members of the opposing teams were expected to shake hands as a sign of respect. But when it came time for George to shake Riker's hand, he held it and squeezed so hard that Riker's fingers curled under one another.

Riker yelped, "What are you doing?"

George grinned naughtily. "Remember the time you tripped me last year and called me a weakling? Well, look who's the weakling now."

Riker's face turned red, and his eyes squinted out a message of doom. Riker was taller than George and weightier too. With one fierce punch to the gut, Riker sent George hurling to the ground.

That was enough to set off the whole of George's team and Riker's. The cricketers became martial artists and wrestlers. The kicks and the clenched rolling on the ground was spectacular and might have continued all afternoon if Simon and the coaches had not worked hard to calm things down.

The "he started it!" accusations began to roll off everyone's tongue, but the coaches were not interested. Both teams were ordered to go to the changing room.

Later that day, when Simon and George were sitting together in the living room at Simon's home, George said, "I'm sorry I started that fight. Why didn't you fight too?"

Simon asked, "What good would that have done?"

"Well, not much I suppose," George said, "but we were all fighting except you. How come you didn't get angry like the rest of us?"

Simon replied, "It was because of the clothing God gave me."

George's eyebrows rose. "What do you mean by that? God gives people special clothing?"

"Yeah, He does," Simon said. "God gives His people special armour called the armour of God."

George looked Simon over. "Are you messing with me? I don't see any special armour on you, and you were dressed the same as all of us today."

Simon chuckled. "No, I'm not messing with you. This armour is spiritual. It goes over your spirit and soul to protect you and help you fight the wrong thoughts and feelings like those you had today."

George sat up in the couch and scratched his head. "What wrong thoughts and feelings? That Riker fully deserved it."

"You had not forgiven Riker this whole time," Simon said, "and Satan was able to use that against you."

George thought about this. Since that day a year ago when Riker had embarrassed him, George had lived out many scenarios in his mind where he had gotten back at Riker. And now that he had his opportunity, it had caused a mess for both their teams.

George sighed. "I think I need this special armour too. How can I get it?"

Simon was glad to hear this and with great excitement said, "Let's begin with the gospel."

16

Get to Work

I have to work for God just like the priests in the tabernacle did.

The priests in the tabernacle were not called, washed, and dressed simply to stand about gazing into the sky or to sit and do nothing. God put all these things for the priests in place so that they could get to work.

God gave the priests the authority and ability along with all the materials and tools they needed to get the job done. The main job in the tabernacle was making a way for the sins of the people to be separated from them so they could have a relationship with God.

> "Thus you shall separate the children of Israel from their uncleanness, lest they die in their uncleanness when they defile My tabernacle that is among them." (Leviticus 15:31)

So, you may ask, what is my job? What am I to do?

Like the priests in the tabernacle, I am to answer the call, get washed, get dressed, and get to work. I am to use all the talents and gifts God has given me, and I am to put on the whole armour of God so that I can carry the message of the gospel of peace wherever I go.

I can spread this message by living in a way that is opposite to those who do not have salvation. I do this through the things I say and do and the way I treat those at home or school, in extracurricular activities, and anywhere I visit.

I can also spread this message by telling others who Jesus is and why they need Him. And I can tell them how it has been for me having Jesus as my Saviour and Lord.

Satan will fight against me. He does not want me to take this message to others so that they are saved from him and live lives that are for God and in God. He would like to steal, kill, and destroy as many of God's creation as he can.

In order to work for God, I must know God on the inside. This is why being a home for God is exceedingly important. It is in my acceptance of God as Saviour and Lord that He is able to use me to help the poor, the broken-hearted, the captives, the bound, the ones in ashes, the ones in mourning, and those under the spirit of heaviness.

> The Spirit of the Lord GOD is upon me, because the LORD has anointed me to preach good tidings to the poor; He has sent me to heal the broken-hearted, to proclaim liberty to the captives, and the opening of the prison to those who are bound; to proclaim the acceptable year of the LORD, And the day of vengeance of our God; to comfort all who mourn, to console those who mourn in Zion, to give them beauty for ashes, the oil of joy for mourning, the garment of praise for the spirit of heaviness; that they may be called trees of righteousness, the planting of the LORD, that He may be glorified. (Isaiah 61:1–3)

Zara Works for God

Zara felt at peace on the inside. It had been two years since she received salvation. Zara was spending her summer vacation with her grandparents and was having a wonderful time. She went swimming in the sea almost every morning, and she had her favourite chips and chicken for dinner almost every evening.

"Aren't you tired of chips and chicken?" Grandpa asked.

"No, Grandpa," Zara replied. "They're delicious!"

Grandpa sat carefully into his rocking chair, which was beside Grandma's.

"Zara, I see you've been reading your Bible and praying," Grandma said.

"Yes, I have. I love God," Zara stated.

Grandma peered over the top of her glasses. "That's good, Zara. So what work have you been doing for the Lord?"

"What do you mean?"

Grandpa said, "Have you asked God yet about what He wants you to do so you can spread the gospel?"

Zara's eyes opened wide. She was glad to know God for herself. She hadn't thought about telling others about Jesus. "I never thought about that, Grandpa. I didn't think I would have to do anything except love God and try to be a good person."

Grandma said, "You still have a lot to learn, but you know enough now that you can share with others. Besides that, you have talents that you can use to teach others about Jesus."

"Like what?" Zara asked.

"Like being able to make bracelets and easily making friends."

"How can I use those to teach others about Jesus, Grandma?"

"Tell you what," Grandma said. "You pray about it and let me know what God tells you."

When Zara got back home from her time with her grandparents, she remembered what her grandma said. Then she prayed all that week and asked God how she could work to bring others to know Him.

One day when Zara was making a bracelet, she had an idea. Soon she was making bracelets with letter beads that formed words of messages like HAVE HOPE IN GOD, HAVE FAITH IN GOD, and JESUS SAVES.

Then Zara used her way of easily making friends to spread the bracelet ministry all over her school and within her community. She also spent time talking to others about who God is. Sometimes people didn't want to hear what she said and sometimes they made fun of her but she still kept on working for God.

The next summer, Zara visited her grandparents again, and her grandma and grandpa lit up when they saw the bracelets and heard all the stories of how many of Zara's friends had come to know Jesus.

"It's not always been easy, Grandma," Zara admitted. "Sometimes I wanted to give up, but every time I prayed God would give me the strength to keep on going."

Conclusion

I learnt that I need to have a relationship with Jesus, which begins with salvation. This relationship is kept through personal holiness and separation from thoughts, attitudes, and actions that are against God.

God forgives, cleans, and fills me. He dresses me and makes me ready for all that He calls me to do.

I am glad that I was born for a reason and that I can live a life that pleases God and touches others with His message of life, the Gospel.

Let this always be the prayer of my heart:

> God, thank you for your great love for me, one who would have hated you all my days if you had not sent your Son to be the way, the truth, and the life for me. Increase my understanding of You. Open my spiritual eyes and ears so that I see and hear correctly, being trained by You, the only true God. And let me not be tricked by Satan into calling evil *good*, and good *evil*. God, have your way in and through me. Amen.

Printed in the United States
by Baker & Taylor Publisher Services